Published by
Pelanduk Publications (M) Sdn. Bhd.,
24 Jalan 20/16A, 46300 Petaling Jaya,
Selangor Darul Ehsan, Malaysia.

Address all correspondence to
Pelanduk Publications (M) Sdn. Bhd.,
P.O. Box 8265, 46785 Kelana Jaya,
Selangor Darul Ehsan, Malaysia.

Perpustakaan Negara Malaysia Cataloguing-in-Publication Data

Leading issues in Islamic banking and finance / edited
by Saad Al-Harran.
Includes index
ISBN 967 978 507 6
1. Banks and banking—Religious aspects—Islam.
2. Finance—Religious aspects—Islam. 3. Financial
institution—Malaysia—Religious aspects—Islam.
I. Harran, Saad Abdul Sattar H., 1950–.
332.10917671

Printed in Malaysia by
Academe Art & Printing Services Sdn. Bhd., Lot 14082, Jalan Kuchai Lama,
58200 Kuala Lumpur, Malaysia.

LEADING ISSUES IN

Islamic Banking and Finance

Edited by
SAAD AL-HARRAN

Pelanduk
Publications

Contents

Preface

THE MUSLIM WORLD while approaching the twenty-first century is facing many challenges. The Western financial system is in a real crisis, in that the problems of interest rates and unemployment are on the rise. The East, on the other hand, though experiencing rapid economic growth, has incurred great environmental and social costs, borne mostly by the poorest sectors of the population. Currency speculation, credit card fraud, stock market manipulation and corporate corruption are becoming major characteristics of these economies. In Africa, the problems of poverty, hunger and starvation are rising at alarming rates without any serious effort on the part of the Eastern or Western economic powers to solve them.

From the above scenario, the world financial system has to look for structural changes. A possible alternative is a change towards Islamic finance (partnership financing) based on justice and fairness. Partnership financing will make the financier participate in the risk with the entrepreneur in the business enterprise. The ultimate objectives will be the maximization of the social benefit instead of profit maximization, and the creation of healthier financial institutions to serve the needs of the masses rather than of just a few.

The question will be asked, can Islamic financial institutions, which have been working in the field of banking and finance for more than two decades, take up the challenges and responsibilities of safeguarding mankind from exploitation, unemployment and concentration of wealth in the hands of the few.

Since Islam is a social system imparted by Allah to mankind, and man has accepted the responsibility to be His vicegerent on earth, man will be accountable for his deeds and actions. This argument can also be applied to Islamic financial institutions which should and must play an important role in the world financial system to bring about relevant, positive changes.

Undoubtedly, Islamic banks—and any other Islamic financial institutions—are different than the conventional institutions in terms of their mission and objectives. Therefore, their burden toward society will be more than others, for the following reasons:

a. Islamic banks have a certain philosophical mission in life to achieve. That is, Allah is the creator and ultimate owner of the universe. Institutions (or Man), likewise on earth, has a vicegerency role to play in society. Therefore, Islamic banks are not free to do as they please, rather they have to integrate moral values with economic action. Money and property are thus social tools to achieve social good;
b. To provide credit to those (the poor) who have the talent and the expertise but cannot provide collateral to the conventional institutions to build a grass-root foundation in the society; and
c. To create a harmony in society based on the Islamic concept of sharing and caring in order to achieve economic, financial and political stability.

The above duties assigned to Islamic banks by the Creator of the universe and the real owner of all resources will require them to be:

a. *Leaders*. Islamic banks should lead the corporate sector in terms of responsibility, commitment and hard work to safeguard humanity from exploitation, hatred and unemployment.
b. *Market Oriented*. The operational staff of Islamic banks should be part of the society rather than alien to it. They should work

hard, commit themselves to this mission, and consider that time is a great asset in life that has been given to us by Allah as vicegerents. Undoubtedly, there will be accountability afterwards. Those people should realize that opportunity may come only once and they have to create the market for their products.

c. *Partnership Financiers.* Partnership financing is the only solution to the problem of surplus funds that faces most of the Islamic banks. Through motivation and incentives which will be brought in by partnership financing, corruption will be reduced because people in the enterprise will be partners in the profit or loss, if any.

d. *Investing in Human Development Resources.* Islam focuses on the development of human beings because man is considered to be the vicegerent and active engine for changes in the society.

From the above analyses, the general public will always put the Islamic banks to test to see how far they have succeeded in bringing to those people a decent standard of living. These people (like small entrepreneurs, farmers, fisherman, etc.) have realized that the conventional banking system based on interest and collateral will not serve their needs but only those of the rich. Therefore, they lost hope with these institutions due to the fact that they have been deprived of getting any credit even when they have sound project proposals. These people have been looking forward to the Islamic banking and finance as a model and hope to realize their dreams of implementing their project ideas.

Islamic banks around the world have been in the field of banking and finance for more than two decades. The following questions should be asked:

a. How far have these institutions succeeded in their mission to utilize their funds for the benefit of the general public through long-term Islamic financing (instead of only short-term financing) in order to have an impact in the society?

b. Have the Islamic banks played any role in reducing the rate of poverty and hunger in some of the Muslim countries in Africa?

c. Have these institutions undertaken any market research to understand what the real needs of the people are?

d. Have they succeeded in making credit accessible to the entrepreneurs in the small- and medium-scale industries, especially those who lack the fund, or to the farmers and fisherman who have been exploited by the middlemen and moneylenders?

These are some of the critical questions which need to be assessed very thoroughly by the policymakers of Islamic banking and finance as the Muslim World approaches the twenty-first century. Indeed, it is the history of Islamic banking and finance which will make judgement about the soundness and the viability of these institutions as to how far they have succeeded in realizing their noble objectives.

Saad Al-Harran

Introduction

SAAD AL-HARRAN

THE MAIN OBJECTIVE of this book is to highlight the leading issues that face Islamic financial institutions as the twenty-first century approaches. For the last three decades, Islamic banks tended to concentrate their investment portfolios on short-term financing (*murabaha*) and avoid long term ones. It is estimated that between 80 and 95 per cent of Islamic businesses are short-term *murabaha* financed. This has led to the accusation that the Islamic banking movement has failed to promote the development of the Muslim world by being unwilling to take risks or invest in long-term projects.

The essence of Islamic finance is that money should be used to some productive purpose, and that any investment activity should be in the form of a partnership (*musharakah*) in which the provider of capital, as well as the entrepreneur, share in the risks and rewards of a venture. To realize this, Islamic banks should establish an Islamic consultancy house (ICH) to identify productive investments and if this institution works efficiently it can help to solve the problem of surplus funds which most Islamic banks are facing, especially those in the Gulf region.

To establish a grass-root foundation in the society and to narrow down the rich-poor gap, Islamic banks have a moral and social responsibility towards their economies by investing in long-term projects. This means channelling resources to the people who need them, especially the womenfolk and the poor.

Due to its importance, Chapter 1 opens with a comprehensive deliberation by S. Al-Harran on *musharakah* financing: its concept and applications, where he identifies and defines the various financial instruments available to banks and other institutions under an Islamic economic system. Islam has laid great emphasis on social and economic justice, equity and fair play. These concerns are reflected in the financial instruments devised by early Muslims. The first and foremost instrument of finance is *shirkah* or *musharakah*. It is a partnership between two or more persons who combine their capital or labour for each other's common good. They share the profits and losses equitably and justly. In modern times the partnership can be institutionalized in banks, limited companies and co-operative societies. Further, these can be regulated. In *musharakah*, the distribution of profit is dictated by the inputs made in capital, management or labour and based on a proportion agreed to in advance. On the other hand, losses are to be borne by the partners only on the basis of capital invested. A party which has no capital invested in a project does not have to share in its loss.

It follows that under Islamic principles the banking system has to be essentially equity based. The depositors of the Islamic bank are the shareholders, who cannot be guaranteed a fixed rate of return on their deposits. On the other hand, the borrower is a partner of the bank in an enterprise. The bank enters a partnership on the basis of economic viability and profitability of a project—not on the basis of the creditworthiness of a borrower. It has also been argued that equity financing will be an aid to mobilization of funds and also lead to stability in the economic system. It however must be pointed out that an exhaustive study of stability under an Islamic system needs to be undertaken before definite conclusions can be drawn.

In Chapter 2, Al-Harran examines the need for long-term Islamic financing. Here he analyses the Islamic concept of development which includes moral, spiritual and material aspects. Therefore, the Islamic bank mission has a multidimensional approach based on Islamic principles for the benefit of mankind and gives serious consideration to the total development requirement of the community. The main objectives of Islamic banks are also explained here.

Malaysia could be a good example to apply the concept of long-term Islamic financing by Islamic bank due to the conducive economic, financial and political environment prevailing in the country. It is therefore a time for the policymakers of the corporate sector to utilize the resources for long-term objectives by establishing Islamic investment companies (IICs). The main tasks of the proposed IICs are to identify and select projects, for appraisal and implementation. To ensure success, continued monitoring and following up are essential steps in the right direction.

In Chapter 3, Al-Harran discusses at length the kinds of benefits partnership (*musharakah*) financing will bring especially to the poor to help themselves. This chapter is based on the recent setting up of a special trust fund by the Malaysian government to provide interest-free loans to the hard-core poor. Practical steps which need to be considered for effective utilization of the fund which are listed here, while bearing in mind that the task of alleviation of poverty is not an easy one. However, once the strategy is clear it can play an important role in reducing poverty and helping the poor.

The urgent need to establish rural Islamic investment companies in Malaysia is highlighted by Al-Harran in Chapter 4. To help curb the problem of migration from the rural to urban areas he asserts that credit should be provided to the farmers and the fishermen. He also argues that if a restructuring of the rural economy will be made based on just and fair system, more social and financial prosperity will come to the society. He discusses the problem of why fishermen and farmers have left rural areas and migrated to the large cities. It is indeed mainly due to the frustration and continuous suffering of having no formal credit institutions available in rural areas to serve their needs.

The only solution to these social problems is to establish dynamic Islamic investment companies in the rural areas to serve the needs of the poor fishermen. This process will require a major restructuring of the economy by introducing the new concept of Islamic finance: *musharakah* financing.

Based on the applied research undertaken in two villages from North Terengganu, Malaysia, Al-Harran has constructed an integrated *musharakah* marketing model in Chapter 5. He argues that the model can became an institution for socio-economic reformation and reconstruction and simultaneously help eradicate poverty among the fishermen. The success of any development model is directly correlated to the degree of participation at the grass-root in the development process. Hence, the proposed model is integrated in approach by combining the economic as well as social activities. The model also serves to facilitate the transfer of financial resources from surplus units of community to deficit units.

In Chapter 6, R. Wilson examines whether development finance can be provided in a way which is acceptable to Muslims and if so, whether Bank Islam Malaysia equipped to play a role in such funding. He defines the concepts of development finance and development banking and focuses on the development strategy for the Malaysian economy. He also discusses the Malaysian government's intention to pursue an ambitious industrial development programme that aims at transforming the country into a major manufacturing economy by the year 2020. The financing needs for development are examined and Malaysia's economic development has been helped by the high level of domestic savings in relation to the gross domestic product (GDP). The ratio rose from 23.9 per cent in 1971 to 32.9 per cent by 1980, and since then it remained close to that level, the 1991 figure being 30.4 per cent.

He also assesses the Islamic financial environment in Malaysia in which Islamic banks are more flexible with respect to their liquid asset holdings than conventional banks. They are permitted to hold the investment certificates issued under the 1983 Government Investment Act, as these do not carry interest like bills or bonds. He analyses the growth of deposits and assets of Bank Islam Malaysia and compares it with those of commercial banks. Most deposits with Bank Islam Malaysia were in savings or investment accounts rather than current accounts. Clients appear to have viewed it as a repository for precautionary and savings funds rather than transactions balances.

The distribution of Bank Islam Malaysia funding by sector were examined in which one-third of financing was for housing purchase. Also investments in manufacturing were much greater in proportion compared to most Islamic banks in other Muslim countries, largely reflecting Malaysia's status as a newly industrializing country. Over two thirds of the financing of Bank Islam Malaysia was in the form of deferred payments trade credit (*Bai Bithaman Ajil*).

The financial performance of Bank Islam Malaysia is assessed and special attention given to the bank's profits and dividends over the 1984–1993 period. Wilson also examines the external source of Islamic development finance for Malaysia—the Islamic Development Bank (IDB). Malaysia has not been a major beneficiary of IDB funding as most trade and project financing has involved Middle Eastern and North African countries, and to a lesser extent Pakistan and Bangladesh.

At the end, one challenge from the viewpoint of Islamic development finance is to harness funds from Muslim investors into the stock market. Equity financing is participatory and can therefore accord well with the principles of *mudarabah* and *musharakah*. Therefore, there is a scope for harnessing funds not only from the Bumiputera Muslim investors in Malaysia, but the potential for attracting funds from the Muslim countries of the Middle East should not be ignored. Bank Islam Malaysia should play an important role in demonstrating the commercial viability of Islamic finance.

In Chapter 7, C.S. Wong evaluates the performance of Bank Islam Malaysia Bhd. (BIMB) during 1983–1993. The first part of the chapter has covers the literature review, research methodology, company's profile and its banking operations. The second part concentrates on the evaluation of BIMB performance. The evaluation is based on a few parameters: firstly, in terms of the growth of its deposits and total assets; secondly, on its profits and the returns to its depositors and shareholders;

thirdly, its modes of financing and usage of funds; and finally, on how it discharges its social obligation as an Islamic bank.

Interestingly, when Wong dealt with the mode of financing. It was revealed that the bank's mode of financing *Bai Bithaman Ajil* claimed the highest share of total financing. It increased from 49.1 per cent in 1984 to 78.7 per cent in 1987 and decreased slightly to 73.7 per cent in 1991. However, *mudarabah* financing represents less than 1 per cent throughout the period of 1985 to 1991 with only once at 3.1 per cent in 1984. Similarly, for *musharakah* financing at 1.2 per cent in 1984 to 2.2 per cent in 1986 and since then declined to 0.01 per cent in 1991. He explains why these modes of financing are not popular and puts forward a new proposal of setting up an Islamic investment company and an Islamic consultancy house as was advocated by Al-Harran.

With regard to the social obligation, the BIMB discharges its social obligation through *qard al-hasanah* and *zakat* contributions. Finally, Wong is of the opinion that BIMB achievements is highly commendable though there are some shortcomings in terms of its modes of financing. Therefore, there is a need for continuous evaluation of BIMB in the future as the local banking environment becomes more complex and dynamic.

R. Abdul Kader analyses in great length the market implications for Bank Islam Malaysia in Chapter 8. She focuses on the market for Islamic banking in Malaysia has become more competitive. This is evidenced in the increasing number of conventional banks that have been introducing Islamic counters to capture the Muslim market. This means that BIMB is no longer depending on the religious factor to attract deposits but has to become more aggressive in its marketing approach. Radiah raises the question why in a country whose population is predominantly Muslim, BIMB has only captured a very small share of deposits. Furthermore, she delves into whether Malaysian Muslims are not depositing in the banking system at all or that they do desire banking services but are not primarily motivated to bank with BIMB. She divides the Muslim market into three major segments:

1. The strict or pious Muslims who totally avoid the *riba* banks;
2. The less strict Muslims who hold accounts both at BIMB and the interest-based banks; and
3. The least strict Muslims who only patronize the conventional banks.

The main objectives of her chapter are, firstly, to examine the banking behaviour of the different categories of BIMB customers and determine the factors that have influenced them to bank at BIMB. Secondly, to examine the perception of the Muslim non-depositors of BIMB, to find out why the conventional banks were more preferred and to identify the main reasons which had discouraged them from opening accounts at BIMB. Finally, some conclusions were made in terms of the market implications for BIMB.

The most important market implication that emerges from her finding is the limited ability of BIMB to provide convenience banking to attract patronage from a wider section of the Muslim population. The current package of Islamic banking services offered by Bank Islam does not seem to fulfil the banking needs of these Muslims. Furthermore, BIMB is one of the few banks which does not offer automated teller machines (ATMs) facility to its depositors. Even though the management has announced its intention to install the ATMs in mid-1992 the project is still in its pilot stage.

Radiah feels that BIMB can still create a niche in the market by improving on its corporate image. To many people, the current image of BIMB as an Islamic bank is below expectation especially in the utilization of funds. The bank's concentration on "mark-up financing" and the relatively high mark-up charged has left many Malaysian Muslim disillusioned. The favourable economic and financial environment and the current industrialization policy provide a unique opportunity for BIMB to involve itself in *musharakah* long-term financing. The bank can create a niche in financing small- and medium-scale industries with good projects that are lacking collateral to secure loans from conventional banks. She feels that there is a need to establish a marketing and research and development department by the bank. This is because equity financing requires the bank to be highly selective in the identification of its partners and projects to be financed.

She concludes that the bank need to educate the people about the principles of Islamic banking and finance and the different types of services that can be offered by an Islamic bank. The main challenge for BIMB to create a niche in the Malaysian market would depend on how far it can fulfil the needs of its customers.

In Chapter 9, Al-Harran examines the urgent need to establish an Islamic Consultancy House (ICH) in Malaysia. He raises the following questions:

1. Why is there an urgent need now to utilize the domestic resources for investment purposes?
2. Is Malaysia really in urgent need for foreign investment? Or is it the problem of surplus funds (more than the shortage of capital) which the corporate sector is currently facing?
3. What will be the role of ICH in the utilizing of surplus funds in the corporate sector for financing viable projects to achieve economic and financial independence and realizing the aspirations of Vision 2020?

He assesses the need to utilize the domestic resources in the country for economic development. Capital accumulation should not be the only main goal of the development programme but other factors such as entrepreneurship and training of workers and public administrators are also vital. The problem of surplus funds is also addressed, which can be resolved through the establishment of the ICH.

The role of the proposed institution is to meet the challenges by identifying viable projects and conducting feasibility studies. The philosophy of ICH is laid down—responsibility, accountability, hard work and time value.

In the final analysis, Al-Harran feels that the major challenge that faces Malaysia has not been the shortage of funds, but one of surplus funds. The main difficulty then is to identify sound and financially viable projects.

The importance of marketing research to the corporate sector is examined by Al-Harran in Chapter 10. His line of argument is not only confined to Bank Islam Malaysia Bhd which lacks the expertise to undertake marketing research but also most conventional banks which have underestimated the importance of marketing of their product to the customers. He argues that in the Malaysian context the emphasis of the corporate sector is only on technology alone and nothing else. He questions whether technology would solve human problems or make our life more complicated. Since we are living in the age of human resource development, their needs should be fulfilled if the financial institutions want to stay in the market to be competitive. In Islam, the focal point is the man rather than the capital. Through the proper education and practical training man can generate the capital for economic development. His needs as consumer have to be fulfilled and understood by the financial institutions. This is why marketing research is essential for the corporate sector. He also suggests that to alleviate the problem of lack of marketing research in the corporate sector, policymakers should employ some experts from some of the local universities to undertake the research. The nature of research should be applied and the business student should also be involved in this exercise.

In the eleventh chapter Al-Harran examines the need to establish a small Islamic stock exchange in Malaysia, the current practices at the Kuala Lumpur Stock Exchange as a financial intermediator, and who are the main beneficiaries. He also investigates whether Islam can bring an alternative to the current practices to create a healthy and conductive environment to the stock exchange. A proposal has been suggested to establish a small Islamic stock exchange to cater for the needs of small- and medium-sized enterprises to enable them to raise funds for business expansion.

In the final chapter, Al-Harran proposes a new role for the Muslim business university student in the development of entrepreneurship and small- and medium-sized industries (SMIs) in Malaysia. He contends that in the new era of globalization and competition, the policymakers of the Islamic banks should bring the Muslim business university student to the streamline of the corporate sector. The business student can be utilized to undertake marketing research for the entrepreneur.

He assesses the historical background about the business status in Malaysia. The recent development in terms of the introduction of entrepreneurship to the society to become part of the culture is also explained. Furthermore, the characteristics of the Muslim business university student is examined—leadership, trust, moral values and sharing and caring. Due to these factors, among others, these students must be brought in to the business life. The current problems that face the SMIs is assessed and the new role of the Muslim business university student has been proposed to be considered by the policymakers and the corporate leaders.

Chapter 1

Musharakah Financing: Concept and Applications

SAAD AL-HARRAN

IN THE CONTEMPORARY world there is always a dilemma for the entrepreneur who has a promising idea for a new venture: how is he to raise the capital necessary to launch the venture? Borrowing the money is probably unfeasible. If the normal interest rate is 6 per cent and the venture has a 10 per cent chance of failing within a year, the lender will probably charge an interest of 16 per cent. High interest, plus amortization, will impose heavy fixed costs on the venture from the outset and this will increase the possibility of failure, and in turn the interest rate. Moreover, if the venture's prospects cannot be predicted with reasonable confidence, it will be very difficult even to calculate an appropriate interest rate. The alternative must be for the entrepreneur to admit a partner to the business who is entitled to receive a portion of the profits from the venture, if any, in exchange for contributing the necessary capital to it. The partner's compensation is determined automatically by the fortunes of the business. There is no need to compute an interest rate and there are no fixed costs of debt, the partner will receive his profits only if and when they are earned.

However, Islam aims at establishing a social order where all individuals are united by bonds of brotherhood and affection like members of one single family. This brotherhood is universal and not parochial. It is not bound by any geographical boundaries and encompasses the whole of mankind and not any one family group, tribe or race.

The purpose of this chapter is to thoroughly examine the framework for *musharakah* (equity participation) and other financial instruments of Islamic banks. The chapter is divided into six main sections. The first will define *musharakah* and give its historical background while the second the different types of *musharakah* will be identified. The third section will deal with the conditions of present-day *musharakah* and the fourth analyses equity financing and its channels of investment in an Islamic society. The fifth will identify the steps to be taken to transfer to an equity financing system and the sixth is concerned with the role of equity financing in mobilizing funds and stabilization of the system.

The concept of brotherhood and equal treatment of all individuals in society and before the law is not meaningful unless accompanied by economic justice such that everyone gets his due for his contribution to society or to the social product and that there is no exploitation of one individual by another. The Prophet aptly warned: "Beware of injustice for injustice will be equivalent to darkness on the Day of Judgement." This warning against injustice and exploitation is designed to protect the rights of all individuals in a society (whether consumers, producers or distributors, and whether employers or employees) and to promote general welfare, the ultimate goal of Islam.

Of special significance here is the relationship between the employer and the employee which Islam places in a proper setting and specifies norms for the mutual treatment of both so as to establish justice between them. An employee is entitled to a "just" wage for his contribution to output and it is unlawful for the employer to exploit his employee.

Definition of *Musharakah* and Its Historical Background

Musharakah or *shirkah* is a form of partnership where two or more persons combine either their capital or labour to take on a business venture and sharing the profits, enjoying similar rights and liabilities.

From the very inception of human society, the methods to meet day-to-day needs have been changing with the change of social, economic, scientific, cultural and political circumstances, especially habits, fashion and the standard of living. These methods regulate the commercial activities and vary from place to place and time to time. The Arab society at the time of the rise of Islam had very simple financing methods and forms of business peculiar to that society.

The advent of the Holy Prophet saw the practice of *musharakah* already prevailing over the commercial activities in Arabia. He not only ratified it, but also himself did business on the basis of *musharakah*.[1]

After *Hijra*, the *muhajireen* and the *ansar* were declared by the Prophet to be brothers. Subsequently they joined as partners, in the form of *musharakah*, *muzara* and *musaqat*, in their trading and commercial activities. The nature of their transactions, in the different forms, is identical. The different nomenclature in Arabic refers to diverse activities such as *muzara* in agriculture, *musaqat* in gardening and *musharakah* in trade. The *musharakah* of capital and labour is called *mudarabah*. These four forms were so developed that they became independent institutions and the jurists formed detailed rules about them. There is a consensus of opinion among the jurists of all schools of thought (including Hanfia, Maleki, Shafei, Hanbali and Shia) that *musharakah* is a valid and legitimate contract in Islam. The jurists, however, differ over its form, conditions and other details.

Types of *Musharakah*

Originally *musharakah* or *shirkah* (partnership) was of two types, namely, *shirkah al-milk* (non-contractual partnership) and *shirkah al-uqood* (contractual partnership).

Shirkah al-milk implies co-ownership and comes into existence when two or more persons happen to get joint-ownership of some asset without having entered into a formal partnership agreement; for example, two persons receiving an inheritance or a gift of land or property which may or may not be divisible. The partners have to share the gift, or inherited property or its income, in accordance with their share in it until they decide to divide it. If the property is divisible and the partners still decide to stick together, the *shirkah al-milk* is termed *ikhtiyariyyah* (voluntary). However, if it is indivisible and they are constrained to stay together, the *shirkah al-milk* is characterized as *ijabriyyah* (involuntary).

Shirkah al-uqood can, however, be considered a proper partnership because the parties concerned have willingly entered into a contractual agreement for joint investment and the sharing of profits and risks. The agreement need not necessarily be formal and written, it could be informal and oral. Just as in *mudarabah*, the profits can be shared in any equitably agreed proportion. Losses must, however, be shared in proportion to the capital contribution.

Shirkah al-uqood has been divided in the *fiqh* books into four kinds: *al-mufawadah* (full authority and obligation); *al-inan* (restricted authority and obligation); *al-abdan* (labour, skill and management); and *al-wujuh* (goodwill, creditworthiness and contracts).

In the case of *mufawadah* the partners are adults, equal in their capital contribution, their ability to undertake responsibility and their share of profits and losses. They have full authority to act on behalf of the others and are jointly and severally responsible for the liabilities of their partnership business, provided that such liabilities have been incurred in the ordinary course of business. Thus each partner can act as an agent (*wakil*) for the partnership business and stand as surety or guarantor (*kafil*) for the other partners.

Inan, on the other hand implies that all partners need not be adults or have an equal share in the capital. They are not equally responsible for the management of the business. Accordingly their share in profits may be unequal, but this must be clearly specified in the partnership contract. Their share in losses would of course be in accordance with their capital contributions. Thus in *shirkah al-inan* the partners act would as agents but not as sureties for their colleagues.

Shirkah al-abdan is where the partners contribute their skills and efforts to the management of the business without contributing to the capital. In *shirkah al-wujuh* the partners use their goodwill, their credit-worthiness and their contacts for promoting their business without contributing to the capital.[2] Both these forms for partnership, where the partners do not contribute any capital, would remain confined essentially to small-scale businesses only.

These are of course models. In practice, however, the partners may contribute not only finance but also labour, management and skills, credit and goodwill, although not necessarily equally.

Types of Modern *Musharakah*

The modern business concerns being run on the basis of *musharakah*, as defined above, are as:

a. *Partnerships*. There are regulated by

   i. Partnership rules framed by the government; and
   ii. Business practices prevailing in the business community.

b. *Limited companies*. This type of *musharakah* is strictly controlled by the statutory rules framed by the government. Its commercial activities are, however, influenced by the business practices (*urf*).

c. *Co-operative societies*. This *musharakah* is also governed by statutory rules while its commercial activities are influenced by the practices prevailing in the business community.

The above modern *musharakah* principally resembles *shirkah al-inan*. The details are, however, considerably different due to change of *urf* and other factors including modern commercial techniques, economic conditions and legal requirements. Let us discuss briefly the conditions of *musharakah*, which are those of *shirkah al-inan*. Other types of *musharakah* mentioned by jurists are nearly obsolete nowadays.

Capital to be invested by the partners may be unequal. For most jurists capital should be in the form of currency and not in the form of goods. The condition for capital to be in currency form is only imposed when it was difficult to refer to the goods in terms of currency. This was true in the days of barter systems when the jurists framed the rules, but now goods are generally referred to or accounted for in terms of currency. This condition should, therefore, be waived. In limited companies and co-operative societies the capital is invested in the form of equal units of currency called shares and the intended partners buy as many shares as they wish. This practice has universally been accepted as *urf* and is therefore according to Islamic principles.

Management

Musharakah is run and managed by the will and equal rights of participation of all the partners. Different aspects of *musharakah* business are as follows:

a. Every partner is an agent for the others, as all the partners benefit from the *musharakah* business. When a contract of *musharakah* is made the condition of agency is automatically presumed to be in existence in the contract. The actual possession of a partner over a property of the *musharakah* business is considered as possession of other partners in as much as if a partner purchases half portion of a specific good for himself and half portion thereof for the *musharakah*. When he takes possession of that specific good, this possession will be considered as possession of all the partners. If, however, a partner purchases some goods for himself only, it is exclusively for him and not for the *musharakah* business.
b. Every partner enjoys equal rights in all respects in the absence of any condition to the contrary.
c. Whatsoever condition regarding participation in and administration of the *musharakah* and variation in the share of profit on this ground is valid. The contract of *musharakah* is not invalid on the ground of a condition of non-participation in the *musharakah* business, but on the ground that a share in the profit exists.

d. Every partner has a right to participate actively in the affairs of *musharakah* if he wishes to do so.

In all modern forms of *musharakah*, the partners have equal rights as mentioned above. In limited companies and co-operative societies the shareholders delegate their powers (rights in respect of administration, etc.) to some among themselves to be called directors or given any other appropriate title. In a partnership concern the partners, by a mutual agreement, distribute among themselves their responsibilities, duties and jobs. As mentioned above these practices are valid being *urf* of the business community.

Distribution of Profit

The basis for entitlement to the profits of a *musharakah* are capital, active participation in the *musharakah* business and responsibility. Profits are to be distributed among the partners in business on the basis of proportions settled among themselves in advance. The share of every party in profit must be determined as a proportion or percentage. No fixed amount can be settled for any party.[3]

Limited companies and co-operative societies distribute their profit according to the capital of the shareholders. If any shareholder participates actively in these modern *musharakah* he is paid for it and such payments are regarded as the expenditure of *musharakah*. This is modern *urf* and there is nothing unIslamic in this *urf*.

Liability of Loss

All the jurist are, unanimously, of the view that any loss shall be borne by the partners in proportion to their invested capitals. In all forms of *musharakah* (that is, limited companies, co-operative societies and partnerships) the loss is borne on the basis of capital invested.

There can be little doubt, after the citations above, of the unanimity of the principle. The jurists have categorically laid down that a party which has no capital invested in an enterprise does not have to share its loss. From the explanation of the jurists, it is clear that it is not possible, after investment of capital, to avoid the risk of loss in an enterprise. This is a direct consequence of the prohibition of interest in Islam and is of fundamental importance for our analysis. The jurists point out that this is because of the fact that loss means destruction of a part of the capital and hence, as it occurs, is a liability of the owner of capital alone.

However, according to modern commercial practices the loss does not cut down the respective capitals of the partners or shareholders, but remains as it is in the books of accounts the *musharakah* to be adjusted against future profits. It is pertinent to note that while adjusting the loss against future profits the accounting procedure automatically works in a manner to subsequently bear on the capitals.

Withdrawal of Members

In the early days of Islam the *musharakah* were generally formed on a short-term basis, mostly of a joint-venture type. It was, therefore, quite easy for a partner to withdraw from a *musharakah*. The withdrawal did not create many problems such as the taxation of capital expenditure, the continuous nature of business activities and goodwill. This is why the old jurists did not feel any need to impose restrictions on the withdrawal of a partner, but in the present complicated commercial practices, legal requirements and public control entangle a *musharakah* for a considerable period so deeply and firmly that no partner or shareholder can be absolved of his liability. So according to a modern *urf* the shareholder of a limited company cannot withdraw from it and receive back his capital invested therein. He can, however, sell his share to any person desirous of becoming a shareholder of that company. In a partnership business a partner can be permitted to withdraw and receive his capital back after fulfilling his liabilities as a partner according to the terms and conditions agreed among the partners.

Limited Liability

A distinguishing feature of modern *musharakah* (except in partnerships) is the limited liability of their shareholders. They cannot be held liable for more than the amount of capital they have invested. This requirement makes it necessary to regard the *musharakah* as an entity separate from the individuality of the shareholders. This common *urf* has given way to safe and stable *musharakah* resulting in big commercial organizations and flourishing businesses.[4]

To sum up this section, the *shirkah al-inan*, which implies unequal shares and is recognized by all schools, may tend to be the most popular. In this case, the profits are divided in accordance with a contractually agreed proportion, since the Shariah admits an entitlement to profit arising from a partner's contribution to any of the business assets. However, the Shariah makes it clear that losses are to be shared in proportion to the contribution made to capital. This is because losses, constitute an erosion in equity and must be charged to the capital. If a loss has been incurred in one period, it must be offset against profits in the subsequent periods until the entire loss has been written off and the capital sum restored to its original level. However, until the total loss has been written off, any distribution of "profit" will be considered as an advance to the partners. Accordingly, it would be desirable to build reserves from profits to offset any loses that may be incurred in the future.

The real world situation may be a combination of *mudarabah* and *musharakah* where all partners contribute to the capital but not to the entrepreneurship and management. In this case, profits need not be shared in accordance with capital contributions. They may be shared in any proportion agreed to by the partners, depending on their contribution to the success and profitability of the business.

Equity Financing

Equity financing in an Islamic economy may have to be for either an indefinite period, as it is in the case of the stocks of the joint-stock companies or shares in partnerships, or a definite (short, medium or long) period as in the case of borrowed capital (loans, advances, bonds and debentures). Since borrowed capital would also be on the basis of profit-and-loss sharing and thus not interest based, it would be in the nature of temporary equity financing, and therefore mature on the expiry of the specified period. Such financing would not carry the same connotation as it does in the capitalist economies. It would, like equity capital but unlike *qard al-hasanah*, not enjoy any lien on the assets of the firm.

The inability to secure a lien on the assets of the business financed, possible in the case of interest-based lending, would make the financiers more careful in evaluating the prospects of the business and cautious in providing finance. Moreover, it would be difficult to find medium- or long-term financing in an Islamic economy without sharing the ownership and control of the business. Expansion of the business would hence be closely related to the distribution of ownership and control. Similarly it would not be possible for anyone to earn an income on savings without being willing to share in the risks of business. Thus ownership, fruits and risks of business would become more widely distributed in an Islamic economy than is possible under capitalism.

There are three types of borrowers who are looking for funds to satisfy their financing needs. These are:

a. private sector investors looking for funds to finance their expanding business;
b. private sector borrowers seeking funds to finance their consumption needs; and
c. governments seeking funds to finance their budgetary deficits.

We shall only discuss the subject of private sector equity finance here.

Channels of Equity in an Islamic Society

Islamic banking is equity oriented and the Islamic instruments of financing is ideally based on profit and loss sharing. This would bring a fundamental change in the role of Islamic banks and would convert them from creditors to partners.

The channels that an Islamic equity investment may take in are the same as elsewhere, namely, sole proprietorship, partnership (including both *mudarabah* and *musharakah*) and joint-stock companies. Co-operation can also play an important role in an Islamic economy because of its harmony with the value system of Islam and the valuable contribution it can make to the realization of its goals.

Sole Proprietorship

Generally speaking, in this case the entrepreneur depends essentially on his own finance and management. He may be able to supplement his financial resources by supplier's credits which played an important role in Muslim society in the past and tends to be a major source of short-term capital.

If the sole proprietor needs substantial extra resources on a temporary basis for a specific consignment or for exploiting profitable opportunities, he may raise the necessary finance from individuals or firms or financial institutions on a profit-and-loss sharing basis, in which case his sole proprietorship will merge into the *mudarabah* form of organization. If his need for funds is of a permanent nature, he may consider the entry into his business of other partners and take advantage of the *mudarabah* or *musharakah* forms of partnership, depending on whether he needs merely finance or managerial ability as well to complement his own business talent.

What this implies is that an enterprising businessman in an Islamic society need not be constrained in his ambitions by his own finance. He can still expand his business by securing funds on a profit-and-loss sharing basis. This should actually be better for entrepreneur and the financier in terms of justice: the former does not have to pay a predetermined rate of return irrespective of the outcome of his business, and the latter does not get a low return even when the business is paying high dividends. Since the ultimate outcome of business is uncertain, one or other of the two parties, entrepreneur or financier, suffers from injustice in an interest-based arrangement and Islam wishes to eliminate injustice.

To sum up the sole proprietorship form of business organization, along with *mudarabah* financing, needs to be encouraged as it will help achieve the goals of Islam. It provides self-employment, and enables the entrepreneur to stay in his own town or village, thus helping reduce concentration of population in a few large urban centres.

Partnership

It is the relationship which exists between two or more persons carrying on a business with a common view to profit.

The definition provides us with three requirements for a partnership in that there must be a business, that it must be trading (carrying on), and that it must have the capability of making profits.

Where, at the beginning of a business, one partner provides, say RM5,000 in cash and the other provides the professional skill and expertise to make the venture work it will be a matter for them to decide how the rewards of the business are to be shared out.[6] In the absence of any agreement, no interest will be paid on capital, profits will be divided equally and, in the event of a dissolution, the second partner will be required to bear an equal share of any loss of capital, although he will not be entitled to share in the increase in value of capital unless it has been turned into partnership property.

The distinctive features of the partnership is the right of each of the partners to participate in running the firm and it is this right which gives rise to a number of obligations which partners have towards each other. If it is accepted that each partner participates then it is obviously important that there is a sound relationship between them.

Partnership in an Islamic society may take one of two juristic forms, *mudarabah* or *musharakah.* The Islamic jurists have proposed other forms of partnership to provide credit and finance for agricultural, manufacturing and trading purposes. These are:

a. *Consecutive Partnership.* This instrument of financing is a real innovation on the part of the Islamic banks. The formula is used as a basis for the distribution of profits among depositors, who, in Islamic banks, hold a middle place between shareholders of equity on the one hand and depositors and/or lenders on the other. Consecutive partnership formula, practised by all Islamic banks, considers depositors of one financial year as partners in the proceeds of that financial year, regardless of matching between the periods of projects in which their funds were used. Indeed, even some proceeds pending from previous years, for which accruals or provisions were made, are included in the proceeds of the year in question. On the other hand, some yields corresponding to the said financial year are excluded, if they are not yet due, and left to a future year.

Such an accounting system was necessary to reconcile the depositors' need to withdraw funds, regardless of the liquidation of investment in which their funds are used, with the continuity of the bank's investments which constantly flow in a mixed basket, and the need to make regular accounts every financial year, as an accounting unit for this basket.

b. *Agricultural Partnerships*. Privately owned agricultural land could be exploited in one of the three ways:

   i. Directly by the owner;
   ii. Indirectly by renting it (*ijarah*); and
   iii. Through agricultural partnership.

The two main frameworks in traditional Islamic law for agricultural enterprise are *muzara* (share cropping) and *musaqat* (water partnership or tree-sharing). Both these techniques typically afford a partnership between capital and labour.

a. *Share cropping*. *Muzara* (share cropping or crop partnership) is a contract whereby the landlord puts his agricultural land at the farmer's disposal to farm and the farmer undertakes to give the owner an amount of the agricultural products. This framework is, of course, based on the generally accepted view that there should be a partnership between capital and labour.
b. *Tree-sharing*. A contract is termed *musaqat* (water partnership or tree-sharing) when one person strikes a deal with another

person calling for the latter to trim and water those fruit trees whose fruits are either one's own, or are at his disposal, in exchange for an amount of the fruits, as agreed upon. If such a contract relates to fruitless trees like willows and sycophants, it is not valid. However, it would be valid in such trees as henna whose leaves are used or if those trees whose flowers are used.[7]

☐ A Combination of Sole Proprietorship and Partnership

In practice, business organizations would reflect a combination of sole proprietorship and *mudarabah* or a combination of *musharakah* and *mudarabah*. Not all savers can, or are interested in participating in the management of a business and may be just looking for opportunities to invest their surplus funds for short, medium- or long-term periods. They could in this case make financing available to on-going businesses and share in the profits and losses in accordance with agreed ratios.

☐ Joint-Stock Companies

These constitute along with financial institutions the most convenient form of investment available to a majority of savers, who have neither their own businesses to invest in nor the ability to evaluate running business or become sleeping partners. Corporate shares would be more attractive to them because of the relative ease with which they can acquire them when they wish to invest, or to sell them when they need the liquidity. In the light of Islamic teachings it will however be necessary to reform joint-stock companies to safeguard the interests of shareholders and consumers, and also to reform stock exchanges to ensure that share prices reflect more or less the underlying economic conditions and do not fluctuate erratically in response to speculative forces.

☐ Co-operatives

In addition to the above forms of business organization, which are all profit-oriented, "co-operation", which is service oriented, could make a rich contribution to the realization of the goals of an Islamic economy. With the emphasis of Islam on brotherhood, "co-operation" in its various forms to solve the mutual problems of producers, businesses, consumers, savers and investors should receive considerable emphasis in a Muslim society.

Co-operative societies could render a number of valuable services to members, including temporary financial accommodation when necessary through a mutual fund, the economies of bulk purchases and sales, maintenance facilities, advisory services, assistance or training for solving management and technical problems, and mutual insurance. Co-operation is a mutually beneficial relationship for all concerned, and everyone's participation is completely voluntary.[8]

Informal co-operation between craftsmen and businesses is quite widespread in Muslim history. In all these diverse forms of informal co-operation, businesses rendered services to each other without receiving any profit, commission or remuneration. These different forms reflected not only Islamic brotherhood and mutual trust but also fulfilled the common needs of businessmen on a mutually co-operative basis.

Historical experience has shown that during the *jahiliyyah* (pre-Islamic) period, trade (over many territories) stretched over long distances and all financial resources were mobilized on the basis of either interest or *mudarabah* and *musharakah*. Islam, however, abolished the interest basis and organized the entire production and trade on the basis of *mudarabah* and *musharakah*. With the abolition of interest, economic activity in the Muslim world did not suffer any decline. In fact there was increased prosperity.

A combination of several economic and political factors, including the ability to mobilize sufficient financial resources, were mainly responsible for this prosperity. All these factors together provided a great boost to trade which flourished from Morocco and Spain in the west, to India and China in the east, Central Asia in the north, and Africa in the south. Therefore, the economic prosperity in the Muslim world had made possible a development of industrial skill which brought the artistic value of the products to an unequalled height.

Mudarabah and *musharakah* were the basic methods, by which financial resources were mobilized and combined with entrepreneurial and managerial skills for purposes of expanding long-distance trade and supporting crafts and manufacture. They fulfilled the needs of commerce and industry and enabled them to thrive to the optimum level given the prevailing technological environment.

Steps to an Equity Financing System

It was mentioned earlier that to abolish interest implies that all businesses in Muslim countries, including industry and agriculture, currently operating on the basis of a mix of equity and interest-based loans, would have to become primarily equity-based.

This requires that all financial needs of a permanent nature, whether for fixed or working capital, should normally be expected to come out of equity capital in an Islamic economy. This broader equity-capital base may be supported to the extent necessary by medium- and long-term *mudarabah* advances. Short-term loan financing, even though in a profit-and-loss sharing framework, may be resorted to only for bridge-financing or temporary shortage of liquidity resulting from seasonal peaks in business for which purpose it may not be desirable or feasible to have a permanent increase in equity.

A number of steps would need to be taken to bring about the transformation to an equity-based financing system in the gradual Islamization of the economy of Muslim countries.

First, projects should be selected for funding through partnerships primarily on the basis of their expected profitability rather than the creditworthiness or solvency of the borrower.[9] This factor, together with the predominance of equity markets and the absence of debt markets, has led Muslim scholars to conclude that, potentially, in an Islamic system, there would be

a. A greater number and variety of investment projects that would be seeking financing;
b. A more cautious, selective, and perhaps more efficient project selection by the savers and investors; and
c. A greater involvement by the public in investment and entrepreneurial activities, particularly as private equity markets develop.

Second, to enable firms to increase their equity it may be necessary to "regularize" the existing stock of "black" money (arising from tax evasion), the major outlet for which currently is mainly capital outflows or conspicuous consumption. This move should help draw a substantial volume of such funds into the fold of investment. Without this move it may be difficult to increase equity because there may not be a sufficient volume of "white" money in the economy for this purpose.

Third, tax laws should be revised to treat interest payments in the same way as dividends and profits are now being treated, and taxes should be levied on gross profits before interest payments. In fact, it would be desirable to impose a higher rate of tax on the interest portion of the gross income than that applied to profits to accelerate the transformation to an equity-based financing structure.

Fourth, the tax structure of Muslim countries should be streamlined to ensure that it does not discourage investment and channel even legally earned profits into "black" money. While Islam does allow the levying of taxes to a reasonable extent to meet all necessary and desirable state expenditures, it does not permit an unjust tax structure which penalizes honesty and creates the unIslamic tendency of evading taxes.

Finally, the formation of appropriate financial institutions and investment banks should be encouraged to make venture capital available to businesses and industries, thus enabling them to undertake necessary investments. In the process they would also provide investment opportunities to savers who are either unable to find lucrative opportunities, for direct investment, or are unable to locate *mudarib* (partners) for profitable investment of their savings.

The Role of Equity Financing

Given Islam's emphasis on equity financing, there should be a greater urge to save for investment in one's own business. If there are profitable opportunities for investment which cannot be exploited by reliance merely on internal cashflows, access could be had for premises, equipment and supplies through leasing, *murabaha* or *bai muajjal*, and supplier's credits. Businesses desiring further expansion could also mobilize resources on the basis of profit, *mudarabah* or *musharakah*. Market forces will take care of those who act in a self-defeating manner. Nevertheless, a state-regulated proper auditing system can be instituted to safeguard the interest of investors.

Joint-stock companies should also play an important role in an Islamic economy. Their shares would be available to investors who are not active or do not wish to make their funds available to sole proprietors or partnerships. Corporate equities constitute a substantial proportion of total capital formation in capitalist societies.

In an Islamic economy, it is always possible for an individual investor to diversify and reduce his risk by making financial institutions and investment trusts a vehicle for his investment because such institutions diversify their own risk by properly regulating their exposure to different sectors of the economy as do individuals and firms. It must be clearly understood that the return on equity in an Islamic economy will not be equal to just "profit" but will rather be the sum of what constitutes "interest plus profit" in the capitalist economy and is called "return on capital". It will include the reward for saving and risk-taking, on the one hand, and entrepreneurship, management and innovation, on the other.

Hence the Islamic system should be able to ensure justice between the entrepreneur and the financier. No one would be assured of a predetermined rate of return. One must participate in the risk and share in the outcome of the business. This may not necessarily change the total outcome. It would no doubt change the distribution of the total outcome in accordance with the Islamic norm of socio-economic justice. It would also eliminate the erratic and irrational fluctuation between the shares of the savers or financiers and the entrepreneurs. Hence situations where either the savers suffer (if interest is low and profit is high) or the entrepreneurs suffer (if interest is high and profit is low or negative) would be eliminated and justice established between the two. The impact of this should be healthy on both savers and entrepreneurs.

When it comes to the question of stability, it must be realized that the stability of any economic system may be evaluated either empirically or analytically. Empirically, the simulation of an econometric model of a given economy has been successfully tried to evaluate stability. The results of such investigations, however, lack the generality of analytical results.[10] Furthermore, this approach cannot be employed in the present case since a full-fledged Islamic economic system does not as yet exist.

Analytical methods of examining stability have also been developed by economists and have provided important general results. Such methods have not yet been applied to study an Islamic economy and have in any case their own limitations. More importantly, stability is quite responsive to government action and regulations, hence a definitive analysis requires the specification of several institutional details.

All things considered, there appears to be room for offering some remarks on the stability of an equity-based Islamic economy. The profit element in such a system will be dependent on the profit-sharing ratio and the ultimate outcome of the business. The share of profit of the entrepreneur or financier cannot fluctuate violently from month to month. Furthermore, the distribution of the total return on capital (that is, profit plus interest) between the entrepreneur and the financier would be determined more equitable by economic considerations and not by speculative financial market forces. In case of dividends it can however, be reduced in bad times and, in extreme situations, even passed. So the burden of finance by shares is less. There is no doubt that in good times an increased in dividends would be expected, but it is precisely in such times that the burden of higher dividend can be borne. This factor should tend to have the effect of substantially reducing business failures, and in turn dampening, rather than accentuating, economic instability. Minsky argues that when each firm finances its own cashflow and plans to invest its own retained profits, there is no problem of effective demand, the financial system is robust and investment has great inertia. When firms can raise outside finance direct from renters or through the banks, they are liable to instability. Schemes of investment are planned that are viable only if the overall rate of investment continues to rise. A fragile debt structure is built up. When the acceleration in the rate of investment tapers off, some businesses would find their current receipts less than their current obligations, and a financial collapse may occur.[11] During a boom, equity-holders experience capital gains and increase in the ratio of expenditure to income; when the boom breaks, thriftiness increases. This long-run average growth may occur in cycles.

Interest rate volatility has defeated all efforts to restore stability to exchange rates. In a fixed parity system it is impossible to keep the exchange rates pegged because of the movement of 'hot money' to take advantage of interest rate differentials. The effort to keep the exchange rate pegged leads to a significant loss of central bank reserves and impairs confidence in the strength of the currency. In a floating exchange rate system, where the rate tries to find its own equilibrium level and fluctuate excessively from day to day in response to international interest rate movements bearing no relationship to underlying economic conditions, it becomes difficult to predict exchange rates. This renders long-term planning almost impossible. A country facing a recession is unable to keep its interest rates low because such a policy leads to an outflow of funds, depreciates the exchange rate of its currency, and raises the cost of living.[12] To prevent an even deeper plunge in the value of its currency, the recession-ridden country is forced to maintain interest rates at a higher level than dictated by the need for recovery. This, in turn, slows down the recovery and undermines confidence in the government.

The elimination of interest and its replacement by profit-and-loss sharing would not only change the level of uncertainty but also redistribute the consequences of uncertainty to all parties of a business. It would moreover, by removing the daily destabilizing influence of fluctuating interest rates, bring about a commitment of funds for a longer period and also introduce a discipline in investment decisions. In such an environment the strength or weakness of a currency would tend to depend on the underlying strength of the economy, particularly the rate of inflation, and exchange rates. Accompanied by the Islamic emphasis on internal stability in the value of money, exchange rates should prove to be more stable because all other factors influencing exchange rates, such as cyclical developments, structural imbalances and differences in growth rates, are of a long-run nature and influence expectations about long-term trends in exchange rates.

Moreover, in the Islamic system, there will also be a greater interdependence and a closer relationship between investment and deposit yields because banks can primarily accept investment deposits on the basis of profit sharing and can provide funds to the enterprises on the same basis. Due to the fact that the return to liabilities will be a direct function of the return to asset portfolios and also because assets are created in response to investment opportunities in the real sector, the return to financing is removed from the cost side and relegated to the profit side, thereby allowing the rate of return to financing to be determined by productivity in the real sector. It will be the real sector that determines the rate of return to the financial sector in the Islamic financial system rather than the other way around. For these reasons, Islamic banking tends to reduce the vulnerability of the capital importing country to fluctuations in the level of capital inflows and to a sharp slowdown of new investments due to uncertainty among investors.

In the Islamic system, no such instability exists when a bank, rather than issuing fixed liabilities, issues shares to its depositors. In this case assets acquired by the banks are transparent to investors, they are no more or less than the deposits supporting them. If there is a decline in the value of the bank's assets then it will not be to the advantage of depositors to withdraw their money because their share would consequently decline. Also the welfare of a depositor does not depend on the actions of other depositors because each gets a share in the bank's value which is independent of whether some withdraw their shares while others do not. In fact there is a greater incentive to remain in the bank when it suffers a decline in the value of its assets because otherwise it will mean acceptance of a loss on initial deposit, whereas retaining shares in the bank will give hope for a revaluation of the bank's assets in the future.[13] Perhaps the greatest advantage of such a system is that it not only resolves the bank's problem of panic among its clients but it also does not require the provision of deposit insurance and other government interventions surrounding banking institutions.

Conclusion

In this chapter, we have argued that *mudarabah* and *musharakah* are the basic methods by which financial resources are mobilized and combined with entrepreneurial and managerial skills for purposes of expanding long-distance trade and supporting crafts and manufacture. They fulfil the needs of commerce and industry and enable them to thrive to the optimum level given the prevailing resource environment. These financial instruments along with others constitute an important feature of both trade and industry and provide a framework for investment in a modern Islamic economy.

To sum up, an Islamic banking system is essentially an equity-based system in which depositors are treated as if they were shareholders of the bank. Consequently, depositors are not guaranteed the nominal value, or a predetermined rate of return, on their deposits. If the bank makes profits then the shareholder (depositor) would be entitled to receive a certain proportion of these profits. On the other hand, if the bank incurs losses the depositor is expected to share in these as well, and receive a negative rate of return. Thus, from the depositor's perspective an Islamic commercial bank is in many respects similar to a mutual fund or investment trust. Furthermore, to remain consistent with religious strictures, the bank cannot charge interest in its lending operations, but has to use special modes of investment and financing that are also based on the concept of profit-and-loss sharing system.

There is no doubt unit trusts and investment trusts are different: the value of shares in an investment trust is determined in the stock market directly, while in the case of a unit trust (or mutual fund) the value is based on a weighted basket of the underlying shares which are traded in the market.

With Islamic deposits, it is not the market value that matters—there is none as they are not traded. Nor is it the underlying value of the assets which the bank has invested in unless there are deposits. What is important is the profitability of the investment. Values of shares do not always reflect profitability. The profit-earning ratio can vary widely, and the market accepts this.

Similarity with unit trusts relates to the uncertainty regarding both returns and the value of Islamic deposits. In practice however value seldom varies, which is not the case with unit trusts where it is determined by the market. In general, Islamic deposits are less risky than unit trust holdings. Income-oriented unit trusts are most easily compared to the Islamic deposits and not those which are growth oriented. In this regard there is much confusion in the Islamic literature on finance.

Notes

1 A.M. Irfani, *Musharakah and its Modern Applications*, paper presented at the Seminar on Islamic Financing Techniques, Islamabad, December 1984, p.2.

2 M.U. Chapra, *Towards a Just Monetary System*, The Islamic Foundation, Leicester, 1985, p.251.

3 M.N. Siddiqi, *Partnership and Profit-sharing in Islamic Law*, The Islamic Foundation, Leicester, 1985, p.22–23.

4 A.M. Irfani, op. cit., pp.23–24.

5 D.M. Qureshi, "The Role of Shariah-based Financial Instruments in a Muslim Country," paper presented at the seminar on "Developing a System of Islamic Financial Instruments," Malaysia, May 1986, p.12.

6 P. Smith, *Essential Business Law of the Family Business*, Sweet & Maxwell, London, 1979, pp.10–28.

7 S.H. Amin, *Islamic Banking and Finance*, Vahid Publications, Iran, 1986, pp.34–35.

8 R. Hessen, "The Modern Corporation and Private Property: A Reappraisal," *Journal of Law and Economics*, XXVI, June 1983, p.287.

9 Z. Iqbal and A. Mirakhor, *Stabilization and Growth in an Open Islamic Economy*, paper presented at the International Seminar on Islamic Economics, Islamabad, August 1987, p.5.

10 M.A. Zarqa, "Stability in an Interest-free Islamic Economy: A Note," *Pakistan Journal of Applied Economics*, II (2), Winter 1983, Pakistan, p.182.

11 H. Minsky, 'Summary of Minsky's Argument' by Joan Robinson in "What are the Questions?," *Journal of Economic Literature*, XV (4) December 1977, p.3,331.

12 M.U. Chapra, op. cit., pp.120–121.

13 W.M. Khan, *Towards an Interest-free Islamic Economic System*, The Islamic Foundation, Leicester & International Association for Islamic Economics, Islamabad, 1985, p.84.

Chapter 2

Time for Long-Term Islamic Financing

SAAD AL-HARRAN

THE ESTABLISHMENT OF Islamic banking and financial corporate entities is a new development in the contemporary corporate world. This is noticeable not only in Muslim countries but also in non-Muslim countries. These institutions provide Islamic services on the basis of a unique and just profit-and-loss sharing principle. However such a novel working system should naturally be accompanied by a number of methodological and operational problems.

The proper diagnosis of these problems is the first step towards ensuring an adequate and efficient working of these institutions. Despite the problems faced by Islamic banks, including the competitive environment in which they exist, they have managed to make steady, and in certain cases even fast, progress. This is not only reflected in the increasing number of Islamic banks and financial institutions, but also in the expanding size of their portfolios. The total assets they manage the world over now exceed US$20 billion. This relatively fast development was not so much due to the religious commitment of their customers as to the nature and results of their financial activities.[1]

In the last two decades, the practice of the majority of Islamic banks shows a widespread preference for *murabaha* (trade financing), and a lesser degree of *mudarabah* financing. And in contrast, *musharakah* (partnership) financing has generally been avoided on the mistaken presumption that it is an economically non-viable (high-risk) instrument. But the experience of the Sudanese Islamic Bank disproves this proposition. Rather, it testifies to the relevance of *musharakah* financing as a tool for rural development and development of the poorer sections of the population. In fact, *musharakah* financing can bring changes and commit the people to work hard (due to the incentive factor) for the betterment of their own lives.

This chapter focuses on a few fundamental issues: firstly, to present briefly the Islamic concept of development; secondly, to define what is an "Islamic bank"; thirdly, to state the main objectives of Islamic banks; and finally, to evaluate their efficiency *vis-à-vis* commercial, savings or investment banks.

The Islamic concept of development has a comprehensive character. It includes moral, spiritual and material aspects. Development becomes a goal- and a value-oriented activity, devoted to the optimization of human well-being in all dimensions—moral and the material, the economic and the social, the spiritual and the physical—which are inseparable. The Islamic bank has a multi-dimensional approach based on Islamic principles for the benefit of mankind and gives serious consideration to the total development requirement of the community. Therefore, the Islamic bank should take this responsibility in the use of funds available. The investment strategy should directly relate to the development of mankind according to Islamic norms. This will require that investments should be to serve long-term development objectives rather than short-term ones. Islam came to show the right path for a good life. It must tackle the problem of developing man in his relationship with God, in his relationship with other human beings, not only in his personal life but in business as well.[2]

An Islamic bank is not just a bank that does not operate under the interest mechanism, it is a bank based on certain economic and philosophical principles. It is an institution dedicated to serve the community and to foster economic welfare for the people and is given to development of human resources based on Islamic values.[3] The main objectives of Islamic banks can be classified as follows:

a. *The Philosophical Principle.* The key belief of Islamic banking is that God is the Creator and Ultimate Owner of the Universe and man, on earth, is His vicegerent. Thus individual property is recognized but it is restrained by the teaching of God. Therefore, Islamic banks are not free to do as they please, but they have to integrate moral values with economic action. Money and property are social tools to achieve the social good. The objective of a bank should not be profit maximization irrespective of the means but maximization of social benefit.

b. *Profit-sharing Investment.* If conventional banks are established to lend money to those who need money with interest, an Islamic bank is established to supply funds on a profit-sharing principle. Without profit sharing an Islamic bank cannot survive. The prohibition of interest from Islamic banking makes direct investment and equity financing a must. This will undoubtedly put great responsibility on Islamic banks since it would then be necessary to make sound feasibility studies for various projects. A partnership teamwork has to be created to identify bankable projects and make them ready for financing. The Islamic bank must achieve high returns to distribute to its shareholders and at the same time maximize social benefit.

c. *Positive Attitude.* The profit-sharing principle of Islamic banks makes it imperative to act in positive ways. An Islamic bank has to go out and search for new opportunities to invest funds available other than just lending the money for short-term gains.

The lending practices of commercial banks, as can be easily seen, is one which usually wait for their customers. Although the concept of marketing has been introduced in the field of banking the lending function is still an intermediate action between those who supply funds (depositors) and those who demand funds for investment (borrowers). Since the Islamic bank is an equity-based institution, it has to go out for joint venture or even for direct long-term investments. All these risk-carrying ventures make sound feasibility studies necessary.

On the other hand, a depositor cannot have a fixed predetermined rate of return on his deposited money. The depositor himself cannot be passive. He has to be alert about the soundness and good management of the banks he chooses. Very often, big depositors once they are advised by an Islamic bank on an investment opportunity, prefer to go into business rather than just waiting for a return. Thus we should expect a positive attitude on the part of depositors and that Islamic banking managers should encourage a positive attitude among depositors and among the members of the society.

d. *Social Nature*. Islamic banks, by nature of their principles, must be social banks, not just banks performing some special social functions. No doubt the social nature of Islamic banking can be seen from the rate of return which must be higher than prevailing rate of interest. This high return for investment account holders is one way to decrease the inequality of the distribution of wealth. This will require more effort from the task-force which will be assigned the responsibility of preparing sound feasibility studies for the Islamic bank to enable it to finance various viable projects.

From the above analysis one can question as to what extent the current Islamic banks have succeeded in achieving the social objectives according to Islamic norms. Undoubtedly the financial gap between short-term financing (through *murabaha* and *mudarabah*) and long-term financing (through *musharakah*) is widening and this has generated much apprehension among the members of the public.

The challenges that face Islamic banks today require major changes in their perception and attitude. Islamic banks should play a major developmental role through their heavy involvement in partnership financing. They have a moral obligation, which makes their role unique and superior to traditional banks, to fulfil in order to alleviate some of the problems that face the Ummah today. This requires more hard work, dedication and investment in human development projects by training those who are the engines for change; Islamic banks can play an active role to promote such projects to develop financial independence and an active entrepreneurship.

The Malaysian leadership has made the economic, financial and political environment suitable to realize this objective. One cannot overlook the importance of Malaysian agricultural sector in the support of greater productivity throughout the economy. There are two ways of how the greater agricultural productivity and output contribute to the economic development. According to Meier these are firstly, by supplying foodstuffs and raw materials to other expanding sectors in the economy and secondly, by providing an "investible surplus" of savings and taxes to support investments in other expanding sectors. Thus the agricultural sector makes it feasible for other sectors to emerge and grow and for international flows for development, just as these other sectors and the international flows make it feasible for the agricultural sector to operate more efficiently as a producing unit and use its product more effectively as a consumer unit.[4]

The Malaysian government has lately adopted a new strategy based on "balanced economic growth." This wise policy means that industrial development in the country should go hand in hand with growth in the agricultural sector. No doubt the policymakers have realized that if food supplies fail to expand in pace with the growth of demand the result is likely to be a substantial rise in food prices leading to discontent among the people and pressure on wage rates with consequent adverse effects on industrial profits, investment and economic growth.

Malaysia is a rich nation in terms of natural resources and the leadership succeeded during the last two decades in utilizing some of these resources for productive purposes, for the benefit of the society as a whole. Others have not yet been exploited due to various factors including the bankers' perception (as the main suppliers of credit) and the attitude of the people (as the utilizers of funds). The government has been encouraging the corporate sector to utilize these resources and to commit themselves for long-term financing. Yet the response (from the corporate sector) has not been as encouraging as it should be, though the government has provided all the necessary support through technical assistance programmes to help the entrepreneurs. Grants have also been extended for preparation of feasibility studies required by the entrepreneurs. The objectives are mainly to create confidence in the entrepreneurs and to support them to move gradually and successfully towards absorbing long-term financing.

The question is why have the bankers not responded to the challenges. Is it because of their perception (that long-term financing is risk oriented and should be avoided) or is it because of the lack of understanding of the project financing concept which is one of the most rapidly growing areas in the field of modern financial management?

This dilemma has to be resolved and this can only be done through the establishment of Islamic Investment Companies (IICs). The task is definitely not an easy one but the initiative must be taken before it is too late. The practical steps to setting up IICs are:

1. *Identification and Selection of the Project.* The project manager who is assigned the responsibility has to select his own staff. The criteria for selection is important to make the project successful. They should be partners, committed to the business, responsible and hard workers for the nation. The government through the Ministry of International Trade and Industry has made the task easier by selecting priority sectors or areas in the economy. For example, small- and medium-scale industries (SMIs) are considered the top priority sector of the economy. Very often we hear that there is a lack of project available for investment in developing countries. The truth is, there is usually no shortage of proposals for projects that have been identified,

but there may be a shortage of projects prepared in sufficient detail to permit implementation.

The project manager and his active partner have to make their own selection based on economic and financial viability—usually done through a feasibility study. The feasibility study should clearly define the objectives of the project. It should explicitly address the question of whether alternative ways to achieve the same objectives may be preferable.

2. *Appraisal.* Usually, when a project is proposed, a critical review or an independent appraisal would be carried out. The active partner should go to the field to do this. This provides an opportunity to re-examine every aspect of the project plan to assess whether the proposal is appropriate and sound before a large sum of money is committed.
3. *Implementation.* The objective of any effort in project planning and analysis is clearly to have a project that can be implemented for the benefit of the society. Financial institutions—both the Islamic and the secular—are very keen to provide credit to the client once they have been convinced that evaluation has been made by the project manager.

No doubt, a careful feasibility study conducted by an Islamic consultancy house (ICH) will have to be made available to the Islamic banks, which will not shy away from funding a project once the managements of these bank are convinced that the project is economically viable and financially profitable. If more bankable projects are in the pipeline then the problem of surplus funds will be resolved and the funds will be channelled to productive use. If dividends accrue the managers can distribute the same among their shareholders and investors.

The current problem facing the financial community—for both Islamic and secular institutions—is the lack of viable projects, which has caused these institutions to accumulate huge surplus funds. If this problem cannot be resolved by Islamic financial institutions in Malaysia, through creating viable projects ready for financing, the Islamic banks (or Islamic counters which have recently been established in all commercial banks) are going to face the same problem (of surplus fund) as other Islamic banks in the Gulf countries during the oil boom, where huge asset accumulation occurred when no viable projects to channel those funds were available.

4. *Disbursement of Fund.* Since IICs have a special interest to execute as many projects as possible for the benefit of the society, disbursement should not be a problem. Once the investment bankers are convinced (based on quarterly reports received from the executing agencies) about the progress of the projects disbursements will be made.
5. *Follow Up and Monitoring.* The success or the failure of any project will depend entirely on continual monitoring and following up. In most developing countries, however, monitoring and following up do not take place once a project has taken off. If this practice persists, corruption will increase and the disbursement of funds will be delayed.

In the final analysis, the Malaysian economy is growing rapidly and it is the right time for policymakers to study the new proposal for establishing IICs to play an active role in channelling funds for productive activities. Long-term financing through partnership will surely help the nation progress further and curb capital flight from the country.

Notes

1 Al-Harran, S., Islamic Finance, *Partnership Financing*, Pelanduk Publications, Petaling Jaya, 1993.

2 Al-Hawary, S., *Economic Philosophic Principles of Islamic Banking*, International Institute of Islamic Banking & Economics, Cairo, 1981, pp.25–28.

3 Khurshid, A., *Studies in Islamic Economics*, International Centre for Research in Islamic Economics, King Abdul Aziz University, Jeddah and The Islamic Foundation, London, 1980, pp.178–179.

4 Meier, G.M., *Leading Issues in Economic Development*, Third Edition, Oxford University Press, New York, 1976, pp.563–565.

Chapter 3

Partnership Financing: Self-Help for the Poor

SAAD AL-HARRAN

THE MALAYSIAN GOVERNMENT recently set up a special trust fund to give interest-free loans to the hard-core poor. The hard-core poor is identified as a family of five persons that earns less than RM350 per month. There are three commercial banks which have taken responsibility to provide the interest-free loans to this group: Maybank, Bank Bumiputra Bank and MBF Finance. The interest-free loans given are meant to involve them in small businesses and other economic activities which can help them increase their income.

The creation of this special trust fund is good news indeed, for credit to these people is quite important for survival, especially since we are living in the age of credit. Truly, credit operations have penetrated deeply across the lives of individuals, families, businesses and nations. It is, therefore, a duty of and a challenge to the bankers and financial experts to work out a comprehensive and workable solution to the problem of credit which is the other side of the lending operations based on interest charged under numerous deceptive terms.

The question that needs asking is, what will be the practical steps to effective utilization of the special trust fund. No doubt, the objective must be clear, that is, poverty alleviation in the country. And since the task of alleviation of poverty is scarcely an easy one, the strategy for implementing this programme must be clear. Consider, for instance, the following strategic plan.

☐ Step One

The appointed project manager must identify the poor people. A task-force should be formed and terms of reference should be clearly defined in order to carry out a feasibility study on the grass-root problems of the poor. This step will help avoid mismanagement of fund allocation even among the poor people. In fact priority must be given to those who are extremely in need of money.

☐ Step Two

Once the above task is accomplished, the project manager should give these loans first to the poorest of the poor because it may be difficult to manage, say 50 per cent of the population. It would be a good idea to initially help 10 per cent of the population. He has to reach out to the poor, who are usually keen to improve their standard of living as they often do have some knowledge and skills and self-disciplined enough to take advantage of good opportunities. Furthermore, they are not as lazy as sometimes perceived.

Lessons of experience from Grameen Bank in Bangladesh suggest that poor people can benefit immensely from a carefully thought-out credit policy. The Grameen Bank has been successful in providing credit for the landless without collateral and retain a repayment record of 98 per cent. Despite the fact that there is a 16 per cent interest imposed by the bank to the loanees, it has been proven that the trust reposed by the bank in them has not been wasted.

☐ Step Three

It is important to identify the suitable project for the target group. One must ask whether it is really socially productive. The project should be evaluated in terms of its benefits. For example, Terengganu which has the highest poverty incidence in Malaysia faces the constraints of traditional methods of fishing and inadequate access to assistance. Moreover, poor support in marketing the products also contributes to a low return on investment. Once their income earning capacity is low, it would be difficult for them to save and accumulate capital for further investment. Hence, there is a pressing need to provide credit facilities for projects in Terengganu.

☐ Step Four

Unless the poor are properly motivated, no system can realize either efficiency in resource use or equity in distribution. To motivate the poor to render their best and utilize the scarce resources with maximum efficiency, it is necessary that their self-interest be served by doing so.

Thus a new concept based on *musharakah* financing is a genuine opportunity to pull themselves out of poverty by means of their own efforts. This concept applies where two or more persons or parties participate in a certain business with a defined amount of capital according to a contract for jointly carrying out the business and for sharing the profits and losses in specified proportions. It consists of an agreement for association, on the condition that the capital and its benefit be common between the two or more parties.

Mudarabah is a kind of *musharakah* (partnership) on the condition that the capital is to be supplied by one, and the labour and work by the other. The owner of the capital is called "*reb'l mal*" and the worker "*mudarab*". In the context of our discussion, the bank can act as a capital provider or "*reb'l mal*" while the workers (in this case, the poor people) will be the partners who will be running the project.

This system will give more confidence and incentive to the poor people to undertake such project which they think is profitable. Ahmed Elnaggar, an expert on Islamic banking wrote on the positive effects of *musharakah* financing in upholding unity and hard work among the society, which are as follows:

a. It achieves a just means of distributing the returns between the investor and the financing agency;

b. It links use of funds directly to social and economic priorities. Since no single rate of interest is given or taken, there is great flexibility in the cost of financing;
c. It directly rewards and provides more incentive to human labour, thereby drawing non-bankable classes into the productive circle of the economy; and
d. It has been tried and proven to achieve a higher rate of return to both parties. This is an incentive for investment in high-risk projects which hold benefit for the society.

☐ Step Five

The manager should make the credit application process simpler and easier. The credit process should not create difficulties for the target group. In the informal sector in most developing countries where the moneylenders play an active role in extending credit to poor farmers, the application procedure for credit is quite simple: the borrowers merely talk directly to the lenders about their financial needs. There are usually no forms to fill out, no references to submit, no land titles to present, no taxes to pay or stamps to buy.

The main purpose for extending loan is to allow the poor family to be self-reliant through the small income-generating project. Thus the loan given should be used as the capital to start a business.

After giving an opportunity to poor families to have their own businesses, the next step then is to raise their standard of living. This can be done by ensuring that the income received from the businesses can satisfy their basic needs and help them get better education and be healthy.

☐ Step Six

The project manager should group them together, and appoint group leaders. This is because collective work can yield more benefits. There must be weekly meetings to look into the progress of each participant. The group should be motivated through the introduction of partnership financing concept. Any profit or loss will be shared among the parties. In this way every participant will be likely to feel responsible for any shortcoming in the project. A full commitment from all parties is needed for the success of the project.

☐ Step Seven

Monitoring and evaluation (M&E) is basically seen as a tool of project management for effective implementation and better planning and is indeed vital for effective utilization of the interest-free loans. The primary reasons for monitoring are:

a. To keep track of project progress;
b. To provide feedback on the project management;
c. To serve as a "warning" mechanism for project management; and
d. To help prevent or solve problems encountered during project implementation.

According to the International Fund for Agricultural Development (IFAD), the Mid-Term Evaluations have found that M&E arrangements at various levels have been slow in developing and demonstrating their usefulness to project management. This situation can be attributed to a number of reasons, such as a lack of trained monitoring and evaluation staff, lack of training facilities for new staff, and difficulties in retaining trained staff in the absence of good career development prospects.

Conclusion

Finally, one can say that in view of the steps taken to utilize this fund effectively by looking at the present Malaysian economic system, there is a special need for establishing a financial institution to help the poor by giving financial support. Such a support is invaluable for sustaining socio-economic development in rural Malaysia.

The operation of bank or any institutions must be based on *musharakah* financing without interest. Hence the system of profit sharing will be able not only to bring about greater efficiency in the allocation of resources but also reduce the concentration of wealth and power. The proposed bank for the poor in Malaysia would then become a strong force for socio-economic change and development.

Chapter 4

Rural Islamic Investment Companies

SAAD AL-HARRAN

THE MALAYSIAN GOVERNMENT'S sound economic and financial policies and political maturity have played an important role to achieve a fair and balanced budget for 1994. The main objectives of the 1994 Budget according to Finance Minister Anwar Ibrahim are economic growth, reducing inflation, enhancing skills and technological advancement and fostering a balanced and equitable distribution of wealth in the society.

This chapter intends to enquire the local policymakers concerning the 1994 budget as to what practical steps that have been undertaken thus far to achieve an equitable distribution of wealth between the rich urban sector and the poor rural society. There is no denial that the government through its New Economic Policy (NEP) have played a vital role to reduce the rate of poverty from 49.3 per cent in 1970 to 13.6 per cent in 1992. But we are of the opinion that more hard work would need to be done among the rural poor to bring before any real hope can be brought to these 'forgotten' people. The fishermen, the farmers and the rural women are the main engine for change and the real economic growth in the society once they have equal opportunities. If a restructuring of the rural economy will be made based on a just and fair system, more social and financial prosperity will come to the society. Therefore, once a conducive financial environment has been created in the rural economy, the rate of inflation will be further reduced and Malaysia would then indeed be a worthy model for other developing nations in the East to follow. This writer will only be focusing on the current problems of the fishermen and why there is an urgent need to establish rural Islamic investment companies.

If we are responsible and vicegerents of God on earth then it is our duty to understand the grass-root problems of the fisherman when he makes the critical decision to change his vocation and leaves his family and children behind. Is it because of the meagre reward of marketing fish or is it something else? In my earlier applied research, entitled "Marketing Strategy for Rural Poor: An Islamic Prespective," I discovered that the fishermen's problem is not merely a marketing problem but a socio-economic one; a problem which policymakers must critically examine.

Undoubtedly, the fishermen are frustrated and will continue suffering all their lives as long as there is no formal credit institution to serve their needs. Therefore, they have no alternative but to rely on the informal credit system which is mainly controlled by the middlemen and the moneylenders. If they do get credit then they must pay very high rates of interest—and very often these can reach 60–70 per cent, as in some African countries.

The fisherman, like us, needs the credit to work in order to survive and to support his extended families which usually consist of seven to nine children. The informal credit system in the rural area is without question unfair and unjust and has played—and will continues to do so for many years to come—a vital role in encouraging the Malaysian fishermen to go for other jobs in urban areas.

Therefore, should we put the whole blame on the informal credit sector only or on the formal one? Actually, both should be blamed. Still, the formal credit system is meant to serve the needs of the urban society only. Furthermore, it is not meant to go beyond that because it was set up to serve the needs of the people in the cities and to create a consumer society—through the credit card system—rather than a productive one. For instance, according to the experience of Bank Islam Malaysia, the last decade has shown a widespread preference for *murabaha* (trade financing), and a lesser degree of preference for *mudarabah* financing. Since these modes of financing are short term in nature and such operations will not bring any social benefit to a large segment of the society. In contrast, *musharakah* (partnership) financing has mostly been avoided due to the mistaken presumption that it is an economically non-viable (high-risk) instrument. However, if the concept of project financing were introduced in the corporate sector these institutions will not have the problems of huge surplus funds. Project financing requires hard work, commitment and responsibility in identifying viable projects to bring real change in the society, not only in the urban area but also rural economy.

It has been due to the above situation and the absence of formal financial institutions to serve the need of the rural society that the informal credit system has come to play its powerful and exploitative role in the rural areas. Thus, the poor fishermen and farmers have no alternative but to deal with them. Is it really fair and just that the fishermen who work extremely hard for survival yet are taken advantages of and left in debt all their lives? If we are responsible people, who understand our mission in life as vicegerents of God on earth, then we should not leave matters to worsen but should create an alternative system based on practices and regulations that are just and fair. What then will be the alternative system to the unhealthy environment prevailing in our rural society which has played a major role in increasing the prices of agricultural commodities and subsequently increasing the rate of inflation?

The solution is to establish new, dynamic Islamic investment companies in the rural areas to serve the needs of the poor fishermen. This process will require a major restructuring of the economy and, more specifically, the financial system through the introduction of a new concept of Islamic finance: *musharakah* financing in the rural economy. Thus, in the new hope equation, the poor fishermen will be partners with the investment banks, sharing the profits and losses. Through the incentive system which partnership financing will bring, the fishermen will learn their duties in business because their success or failure depends fully on their efforts. Partnership financing can help make the poor fishermen financially independent, decent human beings and entrepreneurs through time. Societal harmony will be fostered due to the co-operation between the parties.

Once the new system (partnership financing) is established there is a need to launch a grant (provided by the government or Permodalan Nasional Bhd.) which will be used as revolving funds, to be loaned out to the new shareholders (fishermen and farmers) as advances for their urgent needs. And once they have accumulated their capital they must repay their loans. The new system has to be closely monitored by specialists who should initiate various development programmes for the fishermen and his family, centring in vocational training, creative and innovative projects.

Long-term financing through *musharakah* will definitely create a healthy and conductive environment in the rural areas. The new system, if successfully monitored, will gradually reduce the exploitative roles of the middlemen and the moneylenders in the rural areas. Also it will play a major role in reducing the prices of agricultural commodities and, in effect, the inflation rate; this will ultimately stabilize the financial and economic system in the country.

Surely, this is the right time for the policymakers to critically examine the new system based on the concept of *musharakah* as long-term policy objectives before it is too late.

Chapter 5

Integrated *Musharakah* Marketing Model

SAAD AL-HARRAN

THE OBJECTIVE OF this chapter is to lay down the *musharakah* model, which was designed not only for material betterment but also spiritual upliftment. The model can become an institution for socio-economic reformation and reconstruction and simultaneously help eradicate poverty among the fishermen. The success of any development model is directly correlated with the degree of participation of the grass-roots in the development process. Hence, this model is integrated in approach through the combination of economic and social activities. The model also serves to facilitate the transfer of financial resources from surplus units of community to deficit units.

The Philosophical Foundation

The *musharakah* marketing model should bring a socio-economic change to the fishermen community. The programme should provide a definite outlook on life. It must be action oriented and comprehensive to be effective for social reconstruction. The project should manifest the following notions:

a. Man is an active agent of change who will be responsible to act according to the framework of divine arrangement;

b. "Change" consists of environmental change and change within the heart and soul of man—attitudes, motivation and commitment for the fulfilment of objectives; and
c. Life is a network of interrelationships and there should be no social disruption and disequilibrium within man and in society.

These are some of the major elements of healthy social change through which Islam wants man and society to move from one height to another.

The model has the following objectives:

a. To provide opportunities and facilities for the poor fishermen to participate in the economy in order to ensure self-dependence;
b. To eradicate poverty in rural areas by ensuring each and every individual will be able to fulfil their basic needs—food, clothing and shelter with sound health and minimum education requirement;
c. To encourage and generate savings among the poor and rural community so as to protect social security and ensure for better future generation together with better social environment and social order; and
d. To lay the foundation towards a more disciplined and responsible nation to protect national security and stability.

In the light of the *musharakah* concept, we can list down some general goals of the model's policy:

a. Human resource development, which would include the inculcation of correct attitudes and aspirations, development of character and personality, education, inculcation of entrepreneurial skills and training in modern fishing techniques which should be based on co-operation and self-reliance;
b. Expansion of production and marketing efforts through efficient and effective methods with priority in fulfilling basic needs;

c. Improvement of the quality of life. The proposed corporation's main effort should be towards raising the standard of living of everyone and towards the achievement of their moral, economic and social welfare. Thus, priority lies on the creation of employment opportunities, system of social security and equitable distribution of income and wealth;[1]

d. Balanced development of different regions and sectors of society; and

e. New technology which should be suited with conditions, needs and aspirations of the poor in the rural area.

The scope of activities should be to

a. Provide capital to the fishermen to purchase boats, fishing equipment, net and also to provide operation fund;

b. Provide capital to the fishermen or their family to set up small businesses based on handicraft and cottage industry or fisheries products;

c. Organize and training courses and provide advisory services to the fishermen; and

d. Promote and encourage saving by the fishermen.

The Marketing Model

It is proposed that the model should incorporate all the parties involved in the Malaysian fishing industry. The model is diagrammatically presented in Figure 5.1.

FIGURE 5.1

***Musharakah* Financing Model**

Fishermen	Boat Owners	Wholesalers/Retailer
Facilitators (Management team and workers)		

It is also proposed that the model should incorporate all the important actors in the Malaysian fishing industry, namely, the fishermen, the wholesalers and the retailers, boat owners and the management teams (facilitators).

In the *musharakah* model, fishermen are viewed as potential assets and active development agents; unlike in the traditional system where they are assumed as passive, unreliable, lacking in motivation and are negative minded.

The Marketing Subsidiary Company

The marketing subsidiary company (MSC) will take over the function of middlemen in the traditional marketing system by giving better prices for their catches and at the same time to promote the fishermen's involvement in the marketing activities to make fishermen self-reliant and independent.

The MSC would be able to offer higher prices to the fishermen because it would be selling the fishes directly to the retailers and wholesalers without going through the various middlemen. All the mark-ups will be accrued to the company.

The marketing subsidiary is responsible to promote new channels for marketing fish such as through wholesale market or export terminals.

The objectives of the MSC would include:

a. To collect and distribute the fishes to various places within the state or outside the state or to be exported to other countries like Singapore and Thailand;
b. To provide the direct link between the producers (fishermen) and the consumers by reducing the role of middlemen;
c. To provide up-to-date information on market prices to the fishermen so that the prices will no longer be easily manipulated by irresponsible middlemen; and
d. To encourage the fishermen to be involved in distribution activities as partners or shareholders of the marketing subsidiary.

Modus Operandi

The scope of production process encompasses all aspects related to improving the methods of fishing, providing boats, equipment and facilities such as ice, transportation, storage and so on. The main aims are to reduce wastage and post-harvest losses besides providing enough supply of fish to meet the demand of consumers.

The *musharakah* corporation through its marketing subsidiary will simultaneously function to solve the marketing problem. The objectives of the subsidiary are:

a. To provide vocational training and education among the members in term of fish marketing;
b. To modernize the fishing industry through the use of appropriate technology;
c. To provide and arrange for marketing facilities;
d. To promote and give assistance in fish marketing; and
e. To provide channels of distribution for marketing of fishermen products such as from handicrafts, by-product and aquaculture industries.

FIGURE 5.2

Marketing Channel of the Proposed Permodalan Nelayan Bumiputera Bhd. (PNBB)[2]

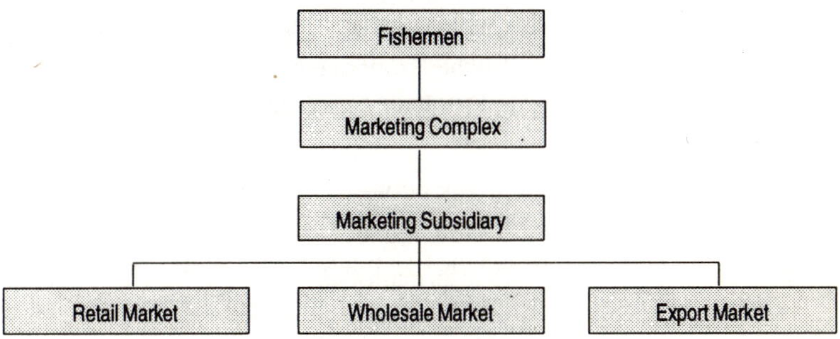

Thus, it is recommended that the MSC should provide the following facilities:

a. Transportation to all the respective markets;
b. Refrigeration; and
c. Warehousing.

Even though, the MSC would be playing the role of a middleman, it would not only become an active competitor in the market but it can stimulate greater participation from the fishermen in marketing activities.

Fishes will be bought from the fishermen at relatively higher prices and sold at market prices at the wholesale, export and retail markets.

The profit is arrived at after deducting the cost of the trips and storage and the price of fish bought from the fishermen. The advantages of this system include:

a. It will reduce the transportation cost by not depending on private or commercial transport owners;
b. It will increase profit because the mark up profit that previously was taken by different middlemen at every stage of distribution will now be accumulated by the company alone;
c. A clear market price will be made known to the fishermen and they will be offered the exact market price if not a higher one. This can be done since the subsidiary company are able to operate in a low-cost manner;
d. The functions of middlemen will be reduced since only the marketing company will be distributing the fishes; and
e. Since the transfer of fishes from one hand of middlemen to another middlemen will be eliminated, the quality of fishes will be less at risk.

For a quantitative example of how the subsidiary company may reduce cost and increase profit in the fish market, see Figures 5.3 and 5.4.

Under the present distribution channel, there are many middlemen, each seeking to acquire a mark-up profit for themselves. Using this system, the middlemen cannot afford to pay fishermen better prices because they themselves are only able to make small profits individually.

FIGURE 5.3
Model: Case of Fish Caught and Brought to Pulau Kambing Jetty, Kuala Terengganu, Malaysia

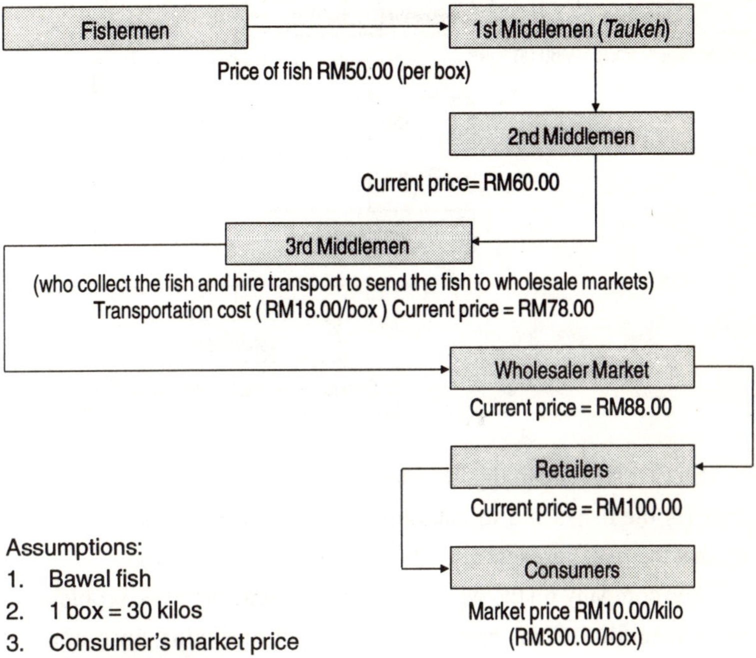

Assumptions:
1. Bawal fish
2. 1 box = 30 kilos
3. Consumer's market price is at RM10.00/kilo (selling price), so RM10.00 x 30 kilos = RM300.00/box

Costs incurred by the whole process shall include transportation cost, commissions or wages for the subsidiary's workers, retailers, wholesalers and managers. If the fish is still sold at RM10.00 per kilo, the revenue one box of fish will bring is RM300.00. The company's profit is the balance after deducting the price of fish bought from the fishermen, and the cost of the distributing process (as mentioned above):

Profit = RM300.00 – RM80.00 – RM100.00
= RM120.00

FIGURE 5.4

Recommended Channel of Distribution under the Proposed Marketing Subsidiary System

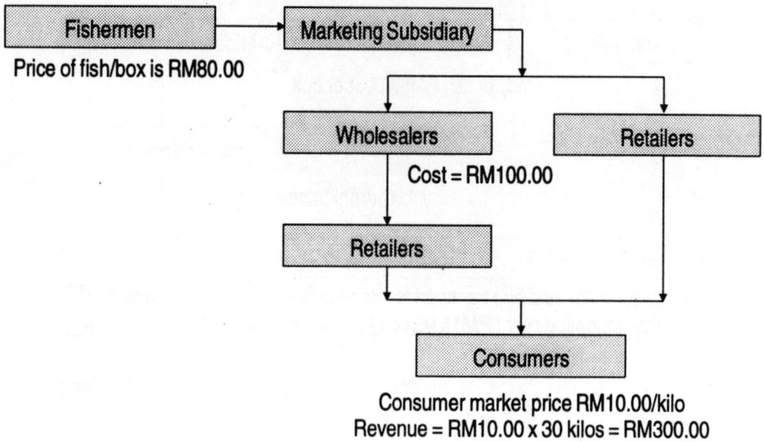

So that will mean that the subsidiary company can offer a higher price for the fishes and still attaining a good profit margin while ensuring that the fishes are less vulnerable to post-harvest losses.

The company on the whole tries to overcome the basic problems of price instability, unnecessary long distribution chains, unscrupulous middlemen, poor quality fish, a high rate of fish wastage and, most importantly, the racial imbalance in the fishery sector.

Integrated Community Development Programme

The other main function of the corporation, is in the area of social development. The programme is called the Integrated Community Development Programme (ICDP).

The programme is felt to be of crucial importance as the success of the whole project depends on how the fishermen perceive their own standard of living and what their level of consciousness is. This is hoped to be achieved through the process of adult education and further reinforced through small group discussions held for each member of the *musharakah* model.

The fishermen and their wives are encouraged to take up various projects deemed feasible towards generating side income or welfare-oriented projects for the benefit of the whole society. More elaborations on ICDP will be provided subsequently.

Entrepreneurship Activities

Perhaps the role of women as income earners can best be enhanced through these projects. The menfolk who do not go out to sea but remain idle at home can also join the projects. The income will help improve their standard of living. Among the areas of potential ventures include:

a. Traditional handicraft: batik, rattan furniture, *mengkuang*- and *pandan*-based industries;
b. Fish by-product industry: *keropok*, salted products, crackers, chips, fillets;
c. Seafood centres at strategic locations;
d. Aquaculture;
e. Fishermen markets and night markets; and
f. Woodcraft and carpentry.

Vocational Training and Education Programmes

The programme seeks to improve the level of education among all walks of the society. For the fishermen's children, the projects suggested are:

a. Pre-school education;
b. Tuition classes;
c. Study groups;
d. Local village library; and
e. Extra-curricular activities such as holiday camps, educational visits and others.

For the fishermen's wives:

a. Cooking and sewing classes; and
b. Home economics education.

For the fishermen:

a. Vocational training;
b. Boat repairing and building; and
c. Deep-sea fishing training scheme.

Figure 5.5
Integrated Community Development Program (ICDP)

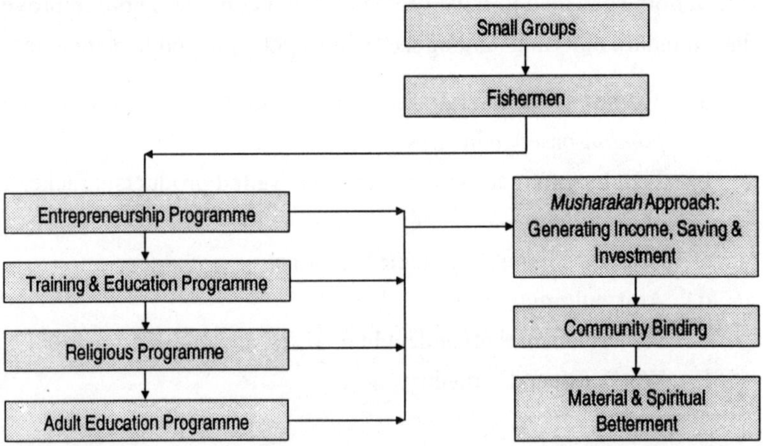

Religious Programmes

Such programmes are intended to bring awareness and create more responsible and committed Muslims. Among those suggested are:

a. Classes for learning the Quran and the role of family institution in Islam; and
b. Commemoration of important Islamic occasions.

It is crucial that all the relevant bodies concerning rural development especially the Village Development and Security Committee (JKKK), LKIM, Fisheries Department, KEMAS, SKN, PN, State Economic Planning Unit and so on should forget their differences and begin to strengthen their acts for the betterment of society and to regain the confidence of the masses. Most of the suggestions highlighted above have actually been made before under the various schemes launched by the Malaysian government, but their success has been far from the targeted levels.

Monitoring of Human Resources

Human beings play a very important role in any organization, whether it is a formal or informal organization, big or small, private or public. A good organizational structure, high-quality resources, and high technology will still fail to help the organization achieve its objectives and goals if it does not have efficient and competent human resources.

The organization should wisely select and give training and explanation to their members regarding the goals of the organization. In general, the organization should pay more attention to their members as creative and dignified human beings. A lot of effort must be put to utilize human resources as an important determinant in economic growth. The fishermen who are mostly poor are also human beings. As human beings and the active agent of growth, they are the one who will exploit natural resources, accumulate capital, build social, economic and political institutions and be the catalysts for the growth process. They also provide important factors of production in the growth process, that is, labour and entrepreneurship.

It is believed that the best way to ensure the success of this program is to monitor human resources more effectively. Under this programme, the fishermen are divided into small groups consisting of not more than ten members. It would be preferable if the members in a group were already related or acquainted so that there will be better communication as they will be able to co-operate better than with strangers.

A group leader should be appointed to help the facilitators or the field staff to manage the group. The facilitator's role is firstly to bind the group members and their families together, guide them in any activities that has been agreed upon by the members, to stimulate discussions regarding their economic conditions and how they could solve it. The facilitators should control the direction of the discussion to instil a critical awareness and motivate the members of the group. Everyone should be allowed to express their views freely. Through the group's weekly meetings, the monitoring and following up task of the organization will also be made easier.

The formation of these small face-to-face groups may be justified on the following basis:

a. It can ensure efficient and effective group binding;
b. It is more easier to identify and solve the problems in a small group;
c. It can provide better monitoring, planning, implementing and controlling;
d. Decentralization of authority will reduce delays and bottlenecks;
e. Leadership skills can be inculcated among the fishermen; and
f. Allows for more efficient and effective management of human resources.

For a better understanding of how the monitoring of human resources model is being done let us take a village that has 200 people as members of the *musharakah* model. They will be divided firstly into two groups: the male group and the female group. The male group will form a Fishermen Association and the female group will be called the Women Association. The diagrammatical representation of the organization structure of the fishermen is shown in Figure 5.6.

The 200 fishermen will be divided into four main groups (MG) where each group will consist of 50 fishermen. The 50 fishermen in the main group will be further divided into five subgroups (SG) consisting of 10 fishermen in each group. There will be a group leader for each main group and subgroup. The leader of the main group will assist the facilitator, who is appointed by the Permodalan Nelayan Bumiputera Bhd. (PNBB), whereas the leader of a subgroup will be selected by the members of the group itself. This type of group division and formation will also apply for the female group.

In the meanwhile, as far as the marketing company is concerned, it is hoped with the fishermen's boosted self-confidence and a high sense of belonging and loyalty, there will not be any default cases in the *musharakah*'s operations.

FIGURE 5.6

The Organizational Structure of the Fishermen Groups

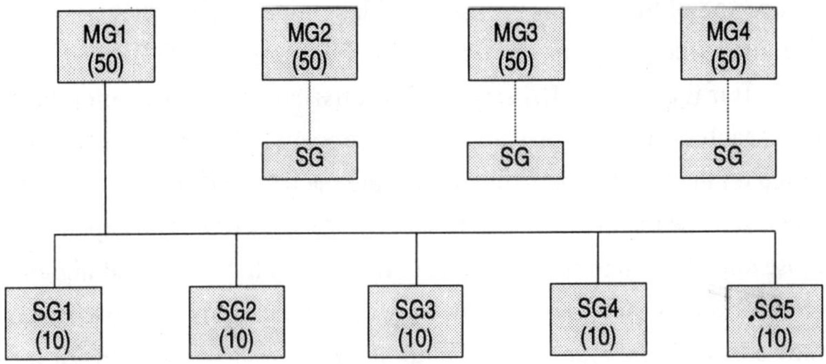

MG (Main Group); SG (Subgroup).

All the group members will go through an intensive training for about one week, conducted by the facilitator of each main group. They will explain all the objectives, rules, programmes, the rights and obligations of the members and other relevant information. At the end of the week, a test of the group members will be conducted to see if they have understood all the rules and procedures.

After the test, during the weekly meetings held, the group will concentrate on group binding activities or discussions apart from their problems and ways to overcome them. Communication skills, critical thinking, motivation and self-confidence are then slowly instilled into the members.

Upon reaching a certain stage of this adult education process, the group may wish to undertake a certain project. During their weekly discussions members will be asked to suggest activities into which they are most interested to venture. Those who have the same interest from all the groups will be gathered and given training, explanation, and various information about the activity they have decided to undertake.

The training will depend on the type of activities and the level of knowledge of the members. During this course a close observation will be given to the member's participation and seriousness as this will be one of the criteria that will be considered when giving loans.

Besides that all these groups will be put under observation for a certain period of time that is necessary to determine whether they are conforming to the discipline and objectives of the proposed PNBB.

After the field staff/facilitator is satisfied, at least two members from each group will be selected to take loans. The selection will be based on the test, the performance during the training, and the commitment of those members. These first two borrowers would be kept under close supervision in the activities that they would be undertaking and close observation regarding how they utilize the funds and how far do they adhere to the repayment conditions. The next two members of the group will only be given the opportunity to apply for the loans once the two first borrowers have reached a satisfying level, and this goes on until all receive their loans. Loans are given either to the individual or groups.

The amount loanable would depend on the size of the project that is most economical and feasible. The borrowers can apply for subsequent loans if they are able to convince PNBB of their project. The facilitators and trainers will always be available to help and guide the members in any of their ventures. The importance of extension facilities and supervision cannot be overemphasized for the success of this programme.

Musharakah Fishing Ventures

The company may also be partners in any project undertaken by the fishermen in their fishing activities. The nature of the company's participation may be: supply of inputs to fishermen, finance purchases of equipment, boats or other capital assets or to provide liquidity at the crucial stage of fishing.

Again the same guidance and supervision is given to the fishermen for them to succeed in their ventures. This is where the difference lies between *musharakah* corporation and other financial institutions. The corporation acts as a partner to the fishermen, so it is necessary for it to ensure in any possible manner that its capital venture will bring in the maximum profit possible. The profit will then be shared by the corporation and the fishermen according to a predetermined ratio.

Conventional banks and financial institutions only provide loans and impose interest on those loans. Furthermore, the process of application and repayment are very complicated and tough that it discourages the fishermen to even think of getting a loan. So, they usually turn to middlemen who can provide them immediate loans with minimum fuss and easy repayment schemes—but at higher interest rates.

Ownership of the Corporation

In the context of the corporation's ownership, it is hoped that the fishermen's share of the capital are provided in the form of advancement given by established financing companies or agencies. Thus a portion of the dividends they get will go to the fishermen as active partners while the rest is used to repay the advancement. At the expiry of the partnership, the portion of capital which is owned by the fishermen, is returned to the fishermen along with the profit.

Conclusion

We are aware that to implement the concept at national level is far too ambitious. Thus, we are in agreement that the model has got to be tested at the micro level first, so that no resources would be wasted unnecessarily and better supervision of the project to identify the potential problems can be made.

But firstly, a lot of consultation has to be done to derive the best strategies based on the experience of other similar projects such as those made by Malaysian Entrepreneurial Development Centre (MEDEC), Pahang State Economic Planning Unit, Amanah Ikhtiar Malaysia, and Lembaga Kemajuan Ikan Malaysia.

Perhaps a committee should be formed as advisers to the institution to help in the process of breaking through the social and political barriers that exist in the target community. Two particular villages are suggested for the pilot project, namely, Pengkalan Atap Village and Mengabang Lekar Village.

It is only wise to implement a small-scale version of the model first in these two villages. This micro version will need further refinements and modifications for its implementation. But it is the best possible method for the 'implementors' to know what it really takes or develop the concept and actualize it at national or state level, because it is here problems, barriers, costs, strengths and opportunities are more easily identified and dealt with accordingly.

Notes

1 S. Al-Harran et al., *Islamic Marketing Strategy: Eradicating Rural Poverty in Malaysia*, chap.8, Pelanduk Publications, Petaling Jaya, 1994.

2 Ibid.

Chapter 6

Islamic Development Finance in Malaysia

RODNEY WILSON

THERE HAVE BEEN several published articles and theses on Bank Islam Malaysia Bhd. (BIMB) but most have concentrated on the institution itself, specifically on Islamic finance as a novel interest-free instrument. The focus of this chapter is on whether development finance can be provided in a way that is acceptable to Muslims, and if such finance is actually needed in a middle income country like Malaysia. The answers to these questions will help the reader determine whether BIMB is equipped to play a role in such funding. Before venturing down the well-trodden path into Islamic financing matters, it is perhaps worth considering what development finance actually involves.

The Concept of Development Banking

The term "development banking" has been increasingly used by economists and specialists in finance from or with an interest in developing countries. Yet there does not appear to be any clear definition about how it differs from other forms of finance. Does it merely refer to all types of finance which are or could be available to developing countries, including external funding as well as finance generated from domestic savings? Should the definition be restricted to grant aid from rich to poorer countries, both bilaterally and through multinational donor agencies?

Such a definition presumably excludes middle income countries such as Malaysia which no longer receive aid of this type. A wider definition might include concessional loans at below market interest rates such as the World Bank's IDA (International Development Assistance) lending or finance from the United States Agency for International Development (USAID). Even this less generous repayable assistance is not given to middle income countries.

For the richer developing countries it is clear that a definition of "development finance" is required, which does not imply a redistribution of income from north to south. Such assistance to the poorest developing countries is usually socially rather than economically motivated in any case, the stress being on meeting the basic needs of the poor through the altruism and "one world" solidarity of the more fortunate with their less fortunate brothers. Worthy though such assistance is, it cannot often be considered as "development finance" as the purpose is to ensure survival, not to promote self-sustaining development. The latter is more likely to occur in middle income developing countries such as Malaysia which already have an adequate infrastructure and a proven track record of several decades of economic growth.

The term "development banking" implies an activity which is commercial in nature rather than being charitable. In other words, the aim is to provide returns for those who put their savings in the bank, and to pay dividends to the bank's shareholders. With charity or alms-giving there is no conflict of interest between the provider and user of the funds, but once commercial considerations are introduced, one party can potentially gain at the other's expense. With ethical financial arrangements, such as those provided by Islamic banks, the aim is to avoid situations where the lender exploits the borrower. Instead the emphasis is on risk sharing, with the bank legitimately benefiting from profitable activity by the user of its funds, but not seeking to impose a double burden on the less successful, who can be driven out of business completely by interest-based banks demanding their full returns, while the equity-holders who have shared the risks, lose their assets. In such circumstances the employees of the failed undertakings may lose their jobs, and the managers, who are often equity-holders themselves, may lose both their assets and their employment.

Development Strategy for the Malaysian Economy

Malaysia has been one of the most rapidly developing economies in Asia in recent years, with a GDP growth rate of 5.6 per cent during 1980–1991, and a per capita GDP growth rate of 2.9 per cent, allowing for the still rapid rate of population growth of 2.6 per cent annually.[1] By 1993 the per capita GDP figure had reached US$3,713,[2] and if an allowance is made for differences in international purchasing power reflecting relative prices, the real GDP per capita figure would be US$6,140 in 1990 according to United Nations' estimates,[3] and probably exceeding US$8,000 by 1994. Malaysia is therefore securely in the middle income economy category, indeed it is near the upper end as US$10,000 is the dividing line into the upper income economies.

The Malaysian government has pursued an ambitious industrial development programme which aims at transforming the country into a major manufacturing economy by the year 2020. Manufacturing output grew by 9.6 per cent annually over the 1980–1991 period,[4] partly due to investments by Japanese multinational companies and technological transfers. Malaysia is a major manufacturer of Sony radios for the worldwide market, and its Proton cars, using Japanese Mitsubishi engines, have proved highly successful in the United Kingdom and other export markets. Such outward-oriented industrialization makes more sense for a country with only 20 million people, which is too limited a market in which to pursue an import substitution policy, or indeed any strategy based on self-sufficiency.

Employment in the manufacturing sector grew by over 63 per cent during 1987–1990 and the value of manufacturing output almost doubled over the 1986–1991 period in real terms. Wages were held in check to maintain international competitiveness, which helped keep export price rises at 10 per cent over the entire 1987–1991 period. The exchange rate has been relatively stable, with a modest depreciation from RM2.58 per US dollar in 1987 to RM2.63 by January 1994. The aim is to control inflation by ensuring that domestic supplies are adequate and by permitting increasingly freer competition from imports. Efforts are being made to further help manufacturing by increasing electricity-generating capacity and investing heavily in education to improve the skills of the work-force.

Under the New Economic Policy (NEP) introduced in 1971 employment opportunities were created for the indigenous Malay population to make them less dependent on agriculture.[5] Many jobs were created by the government, often within the state sector, to ensure the "Bumiputera" majority got a fair share of the national income, as hitherto the Chinese—although constituting only 35 per cent of the population—had dominated the economy through their business activity. State trusts which aimed at providing employment for the Bumiputeras included Perbadanan Nasional Bhd. (PERNAS), Council of Trust for Indigenous People (MARA), Urban Development Authority (UDA), Bumiputra Investment Fund, Bank Bumiputra, Development Bank of Malaysia (BPMB) and National Equity Corporation (PNB). The MARA has a small shareholding in BIMB, the institution which will be discussed later in this chapter.

Just how far these state trusts have developed can be judged by the success of PETRONAS, which in 1996 will move into a new headquarters building consisting of the two highest towers in the world. Each tower has a faceted profile based on Islamic geometry, with unique 16 corner offices which should make the structures one of the world's most elegant buildings, and not merely the largest. These developments symbolize Malaysia's ambitious, yet pragmatic growth strategy. The NEP might have failed, had it merely been about resource shifts to the more needy, but at the time, less productive. As the policy evolved the emphasis shifted to providing better education and training for the Malays, rather than merely exercising positive discrimination in government employment. The aim was to ensure that the Bumiputeras could gain employment themselves in manufacturing and distribution. Hence, by the 1980s trust funds were invested in Chinese as well as Malay businesses, and at the same time the controls on the Chinese business community were relaxed.

Financing Needs for Development

The history of modern commercial banking in Malaysia dates from the nineteenth century, with the British overseas banks involved in the financing of the plantations and rubber and palm-oil exports. As part of the British Empire, the financial system was regulated under English law, although there was much informal moneychanging and moneylending by the Chinese business community. When Singapore got its independence, Malaysia lost its commercial capital; but Kuala Lumpur soon built up its own indigenous financial services sector, and by the 1970s there was an adequate level of commercial banking provision.

Whether the development of a financial infrastructure is a prerequisite for, or a consequence of, development has long been debated. In the case of Malaysia the extent of financial deepening is apparent from the ratio of demand deposits to GDP which rose from 8.1 per cent in 1980 to 14.9 per cent in 1992, or in the wider ratio of time and savings to GDP, which rose from 27.4 per cent in 1980 to 63.1 per cent by 1992. The comparable ratio for the United Kingdom was 146 per cent in 1992; this indicates just how developed the Malaysian financial sector has become.[6]

Malaysia's economic development has been helped by the high level of domestic savings in relation to GDP. The ratio rose from 23.9 per cent in 1971 to 32.9 per cent by 1980, and since then it remained close to that level; the 1991 figure being 30.4 per cent. This is higher than the level of most developing countries, although below the average of 38.2 per cent for the other rapidly growing East Asian economies. For South Korea the ratio was 36.5 per cent for 1991, for China 38.8 per cent and for Singapore a very high ratio of 46.8 per cent. There is, of course, a high correlation between domestic savings ratios and investment, the differences being accounted for by net investment inflows and outflows. For Malaysia the ratio of investment to GDP rose from 22.4 per cent in 1971 to 30.4 per cent in 1980. The rate fluctuated during the 1980s from a high of 37.8 per cent in 1983 to a low of 23.2 per cent in 1987. By 1991 the rate was 35.9 per cent, slightly below the East Asian average of 35.8 per cent, but at par with China, and less than four percentage points below Korea and Thailand.[7]

In these circumstances it could easily be argued that there is no financing gap in Malaysia, and therefore development finance is not really an issue. This may be the case at the macro-economic level, but at the micro-economic level there are gaps. The development of the country has been uneven, with much investment concentrated in the region of the national capital. Furthermore, despite two decades having passed since the New Economic Policy was introduced, many of the Bumiputeras have not participated actively in the development process. Bumiputera individuals still own less than five per cent of the corporate sector, and over one quarter of the rural population is still classified as poor. As a majority of the Bumiputeras are Muslims, it is with respect to this group that there is potentially a clear role for an Islamic bank, and Islamic development finance.

The Islamic Financial Environment in Malaysia

An Islamic Banking Act was passed by the Malaysian parliament in 1983 establishing the law under which these new banks should operate. Under Act 276, anyone wishing to open an Islamic bank has to apply to the Central Bank for a licence, which only it and the Ministry of Finance has the power to grant and revoke.[8] There is some ambiguity in the act regarding the powers of the Central Bank and the Ministry of Finance, although it is clear that the former has technical control, but the minister has the ultimate power of decision making. The Malaysian central bank is still run on the traditional British model, rather than being an independent centre of financial power. The act stipulates that an Islamic bank must maintain a reserve fund of at least 50 per cent of the paid-up capital of the bank, but not more than 100 per cent. The paid-up capital should be not less than 25 per cent of the net profits after taxation and *zakat* (Islamic taxation). This provision effectively sets an upper limit on the dividends that can be paid to shareholders, and implicitly recognizes that there could be a conflict between shareholder and depositor interests.

Islamic banks have greater flexibility with respect to their liquid asset holdings than conventional banks in Malaysia. They are permitted to hold the investment certificates issued under the Government Investment Act 1983, as these do not carry interest like bills or bonds. There is provision for the inclusion of new types of Islamically acceptable assets as part of their liquidity, providing such assets are acceptable to the Central Bank. Apart from this, most of the other legal provisions are the same as those for conventional banks, including those relating to financial reporting, management, take-overs of other banks and loans to employees and directors. There is a maximum of RM10,000 for each unsecured loan, a provision that is included for financial prudence.

In practice the only bank established under the 1983 law was Bank Islam Malaysia. It has enjoyed a virtual monopoly of Islamic banking in Malaysia since its inception in 1984, although the act was not exclusively designed to cater for it, but could also be used to regulate competitors, if any were founded. The Hajj Fund is the only other Islamic financial institution in Malaysia, but it is not a bank. Founded originally as the Pilgrim's Savings Corporation in 1963, it was established so that the Muslims in Malaysia could save on a regular basis to pay for their pilgrimage to Mecca. In 1969 this corporation was merged with the Pilgrim Affairs Administration of the government to form the Pilgrim's Management Fund Board. By 1990 this board had attracted 1,753,678 savers, and its total assets were worth over RM1.2 billion,[9] more than BIMB. This indicates the Muslim savings potential in Malaysia, especially when it is motivated by a religious objective, the desire to make a once in a lifetime pilgrimage to Islam's holiest shrine.

Deposit Growth

Figure 6.1 illustrates the growth of deposits in and assets of BIMB. There was a rapid growth in deposits over the 1984–1987 period, as the concept of Islamic banking attracted Muslim depositors—usually from among those who already had accounts with conventional banks rather than clients who had not acquired the banking habit. Deposit growth then slowed down until 1990, and the following year's deposits actually fell. Did this deposit performance reflect developments in the Malaysian economy or its financial system, or customer perception of the Islamic bank itself, which was once regarded as a "mature" and established institution? During the 1987–1991 period Malaysian GDP growth actually accelerated from 5.4 per cent to 9.7 per cent. The years of economic stagnation had been the mid-1980s, with GDP falling by 1 per cent in 1985 and growing by a mere 1 per cent in 1986.[10] Yet these were the years when BIMB's deposits grew rapidly. It seems there is no correlation between macro-economic performance and that of BIMB.

In contrast there does seem to be a close association between what was happening to the macro-economy and aggregate commercial bank deposits. Demand deposits in Malaysian commercial banks fell by around 1 per cent a year over the 1984–1986 period, and time deposits fell by over 2 per cent annually over the 1984–1987 period. The latter trend may have reflected the fall of over six percentage points on interest on time deposits from 9.5 per cent in 1984 to 3.0 per cent by 1987.[11] When interest rates again rose from 3.8 per cent in 1988 to 7.18 per cent, time deposits also increased, indicating that for Malaysian depositors, at least in the Chinese community if perhaps not for the Bumiputera Muslims, interest rates affect financial behaviour.

For commercial bank demand deposits in aggregate, there appears to be a close association with GDP growth. As such deposits are largely used for transactions purposes, which is not surprising. During the late 1980s and early 1990s when there were high rates of GDP growth as already indicated, demand deposits grew between two and three times as rapidly with the peak of 24.4 per cent in 1989, followed by increases of

FIGURE 6.1
Bank Islam Malaysia: Deposits and Assets

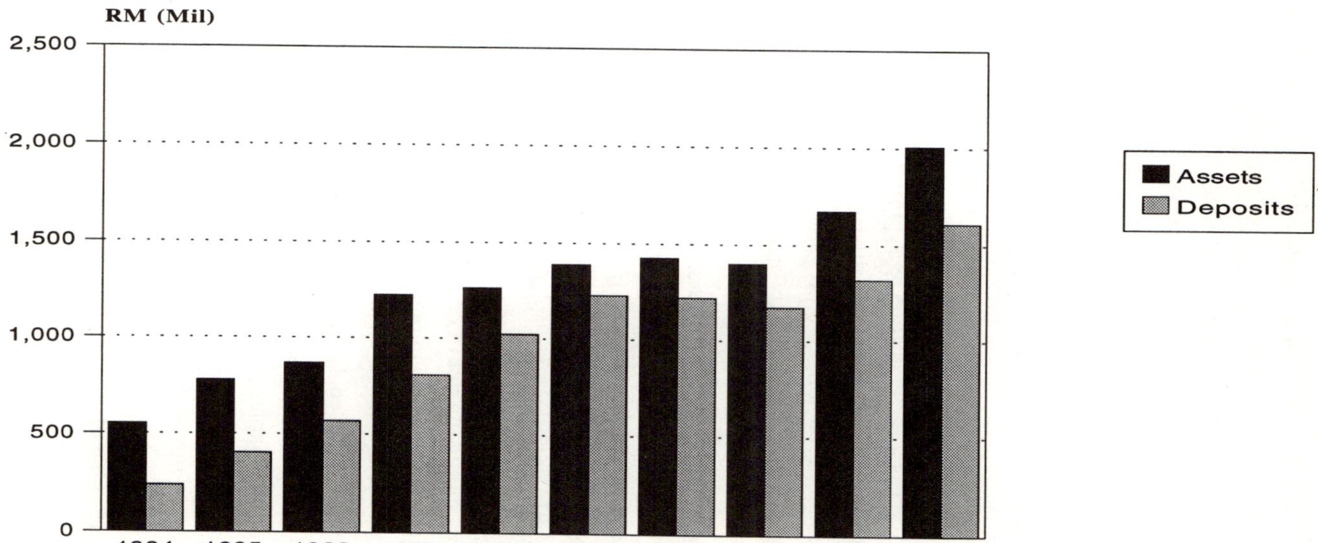

	1984	1985	1986	1987	1988	1989	1990	1991	1992	1993
Assets	551	778	868	1,223	1,263	1,389	1,426	1,400	1,676	2,009
Deposits	241	405	567	809	1,022	1,229	1,221	1,175	1,322	1,612

Sources: BIMB Annual Reports.

17.8 per cent and 11.7 per cent in the two following years. During this period prices were only rising in the 2–4 per cent range annually, which implies that the need to maintain real cash balances was probably not a significant factor explaining transactions deposit growth, but rather the fast pace of real growth.

Most deposits with BIMB were in savings or investment accounts rather than current accounts. Clients appear to have viewed it as a repository for precautionary and savings funds rather than transactions balances. The deposits tended to be regarded as long-term holdings such as savings to cover the deposit on a house, the purchase of a major consumer item such as a car, education fees, pilgrimage expenses, payment for a marriage feast or the cost of health treatment in old age. The bank itself has encouraged longer term rather than short-term deposits through its profit distribution policy on investment accounts. As Figure 6.2 shows, the return on such deposits increased sharply for longer minimum notice of withdrawal periods. Depositors giving five years' or 60 month's notice could obtain twice the return of those giving only one month's notice. Over 70 per cent of investment depositors are at one years' notice or more, as with such lengthy periods the returns compare very favourably with the interest being paid by conventional banks in Malaysia.

Such fine tuning of rates of return according to notice period means it is those depositors who can plan their financial affairs in an orderly fashion who do best. The scope for financial discretion and impulse purchase decisions is reduced, but the aim is to encourage Muslim clients to plan and think long term. The benefit for the bank is a more stable deposit base, which enables its managers to think strategically about their funding policies, rather than being forced to maintain high short-term returns to avoid a run on deposits.

Savings deposits with commercial banks in Malaysia are around four times the value of demand deposits, which demonstrates the concern of bank clients to obtain a return on their funds rather than merely holding idle transactions balances. During the 1970s and early 1980s

FIGURE 6.2
Bank Islam Malaysia: Returns to Depositors

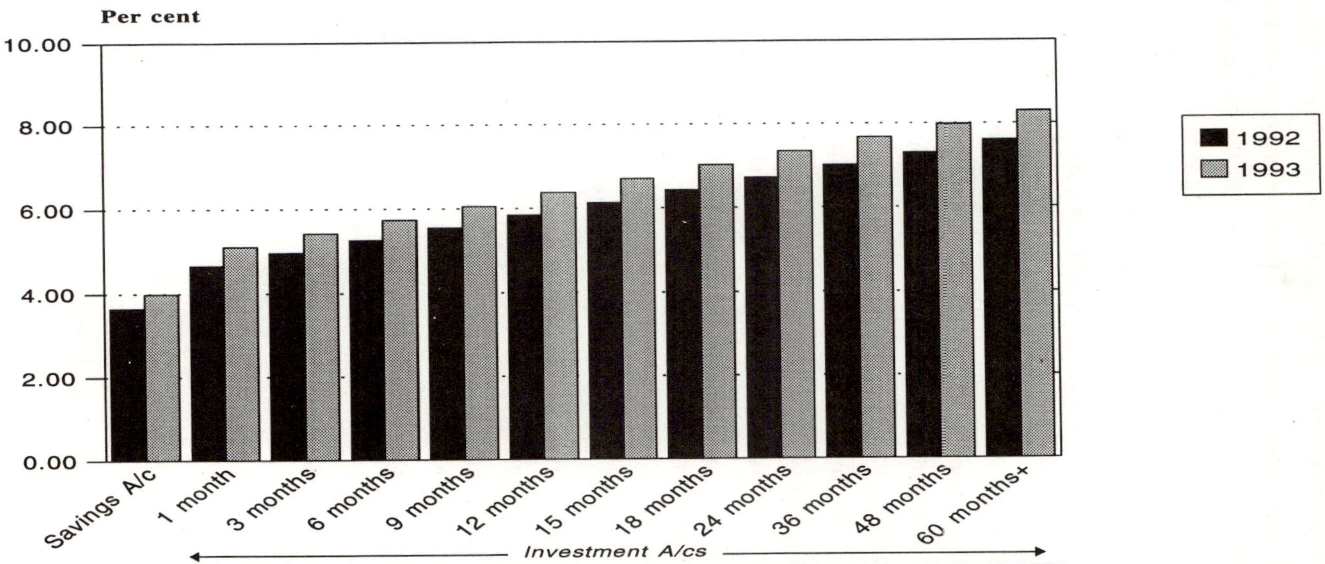

1992	3.65	4.67	4.97	5.26	5.55	5.84	6.13	6.42	6.72	7.01	7.30	7.59
1993	3.99	5.11	5.42	5.74	6.06	6.38	6.70	7.02	7.34	7.66	7.98	8.30

Sources: BIMB Annual Reports.

there was an especially rapid increase in savings deposits, but this tended to slow down in the mid-1980s, and since then the growth of demand deposits has been more rapid, reflecting the desire for liquidity in a rapidly growing economy, not least to be able to take advantage of buying opportunities of the booming Kuala Lumpur Stock Exchange, as well as trading opportunities generally.

In retrospect, it appears that BIMB, as a savings institution primarily, started business at a bad time. Its success in attracting deposits probably lay more in capturing a niche proportion of the market for savings, and appealing to Muslim ethical sentiments, rather than being able to take advantage of an expanded market for savings more generally. This was possible because the bank was a relatively small player in the market, whose share of deposits accounted for less than 1.5 per cent of the total in 1992. Nevertheless its achievement in capturing this share in just eight years of operation is quite remarkable, especially in a situation which favours those established banks that could provide a much wider range of transactions services.

Financing Policy

The distribution of BIMB funding by sector is illustrated in Figure 6.3. One-third of its financing is for housing purchase, indicating the extent to which it is functioning like a United States savings and loan association or a United Kingdom building society rather than a commercial bank. Basically BIMB is a retail financial institution dealing with personal customers and small business clients, and to a much lesser extent Muslim landowners and traders, rather than a big business or a wholesale institution involved with industry and other banks and financial institutions. It has undertaken a relatively large number of financing deals, with over 16,700 outstanding in the 1992–1993 financial year; but this meant an average financing of only RM57,450 (US$21,687). The larger advances were for housing purchase, land acquisition and construction and the smaller amounts for manufacturing and trade.

FIGURE 6.3
Bank Islam Malaysia: Financing

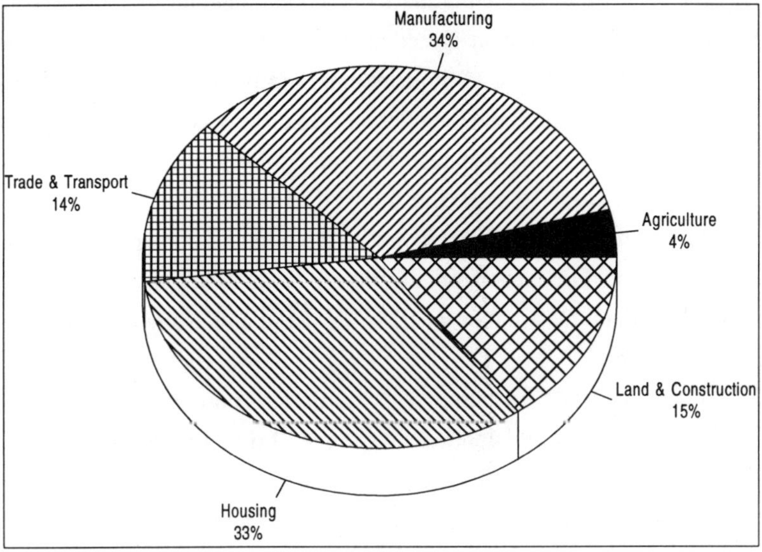

The total financing from July 1992 to June 1993 was RM996.5mil, while the total number of financing accounts was 16,711 in June 1992 compared to 12,456 in July 1991.
Sources: BIMB Reports.

Investments in manufacturing were much greater in proportion to most Islamic banks in other Muslim countries, largely reflecting Malaysia's status as a newly industrializing country. Over one-third of total financing was to support manufacturing as Figure 6.3 shows, whereas a mere 4 per cent was allocated to agricultural projects. Much of the manufacturing financing was to support equipment purchases by small industrial establishments, some of which was financed jointly with other banks. The industries supported usually had the backing of Bumiputera Muslim investors or trust agencies, although many were actually managed by the Chinese business community. Arguably a larger proportion of funding for agriculture would have more directly benefited the Bumiputera, by backing Muslim rural landowners.

Over two-thirds of the financing of BIMB was in the form of *Bai Bithaman Ajil* (deferred payments trade credit). Under this type of funding the bank finances the purchase of a good on behalf of a client, who later repays the bank at an agreed mark-up. The deferred period for the payment is typically one to three months, similar to the period for trade credit from a conventional commercial bank. Bank Islam Malaysia is of course taking on a risk with respect to such financing, as the client may not be in a position to make the deferred payment. It is this risk which justifies its return under Islamic law, as it could be said to be underwriting the client. The fact that the terms are fixed in advance, and freely agreed by all parties, makes the transaction fair and just from an Islamic point of view.

For many trade financing deals *murabaha* contract is used, similar to those employed by Islamic banks in the Middle East and elsewhere. Under this type of financing the bank actually purchases the good on behalf of the client, and then resells it to the client with a mark-up, typically in three or six months time. With such financing there is not only the risk of payments default, as with *Bai Bithaman Ajil*, but there is also the ownership risk associated with having legal title to the goods. The merchandise or equipment may be defective, or could be damaged or lost as a result of an accident. In this case the bank is not merely assuming a financing risk, but is also taking on business risk in association with the handling and use of the good in question. The element of participatory financing is much greater, and there is a real degree of risk sharing.

For longer term financing of one to five years, leasing is the most usual method, following the Islamically acceptable *Ijarah* practice. Around 10 per cent of BIMB finance is on this basis, with the client having the possibility of purchasing the good for a predetermined nominal sum at the end of the leasing period in a type of hire purchase arrangement. The bank owns the goods being leased, but has to depreciate the value of its leased assets each year. It has two options in this respect. One is to take account of the resale market value if the client defaults on the lease, as the longer the time period, the less the secondhand equipment will be worth. The alternative practice, and the method followed by BIMB, is to take account of the reduced number of future payments as the years pass by.

FIGURE 6.4
Bank Islam Malaysia: Methods of Financing

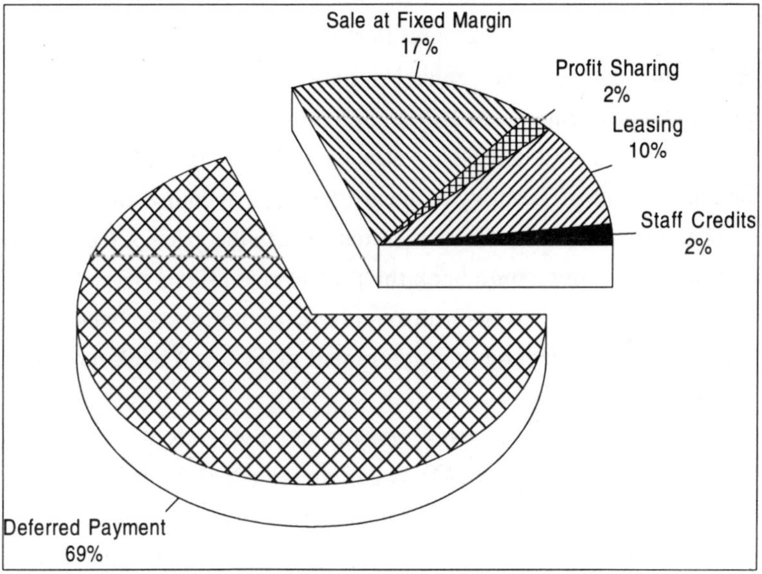

The deferred payment financing was worth RM731mil in 1992–1993. With sales at fixed margins, the bank purchases the goods on the client's behalf and assumes an ownership risk.
Sources: BIMB Reports.

As Figure 6.4 shows there is very little longer term financing through profit sharing with the bank taking an equity stake in the projects being backed using the Islamic *mudarabah* method. This partly reflects the risks associated with such investments as the businesses BIMB backs are usually private concerns not quoted on the Kuala Lumpur Stock Exchange. Disinvestment therefore involves a private sale with perhaps high transactions costs rather than the ease of selling through a stock market. Client demand for *mudarabah* financing would also appear to be limited in Malaysia. Most long-term funding for investment comes from ploughed back profits. Banks tend to be regarded as sources for trade rather than investment finance. Owners of small businesses are concerned about losing control of their family enterprises, and in this respect an Islamic bank is viewed with as much suspicion as any other financing agency.

Financial Performance

As a public company with annual audited accounts, it is possible to appraise the performance of BIMB, and make comparisons over time, especially as over a decade has now passed since the bank started its operations. The profitability of the institution is, of course, of interest to its shareholders, as this affects their returns and the value of their stock. In the case of an Islamic bank the profits also affects the returns to depositors, which contrasts with savers with a conventional bank whose interest rewards depend on government and central bank monetary policy.

Figure 6.5 shows the bank's profits and dividends over the 1984–1993 period, with profits in Malaysian ringgit (RM) shown on the left-hand axis and the percentage dividend on the right-hand axis. The bank made a small loss in its first full year of operation, reflecting the costs in getting started, and the lag in obtaining returns. After that it was profitable, but profits were relatively small until 1988. Since then profits have risen almost six-fold, but from an extremely low base. The rises have been rather uneven, but nevertheless impressive, with an increase every year. To some extent this reflected the substantial growth of the Malaysian economy, but it also indicates sound management within the bank.

Dividend payments have increased in line with profits, but in settling dividends the directors of the bank also take account of dividends paid by other banks to their shareholders, as well as returns to investors in Malaysia. In the case of Islamic banks there is a trade-off between payments to shareholders and the profits to depositors. A larger payment to the latter means smaller returns to the former. On the other hand,

FIGURE 6.5
Bank Islam Malaysia: Profits and Dividends

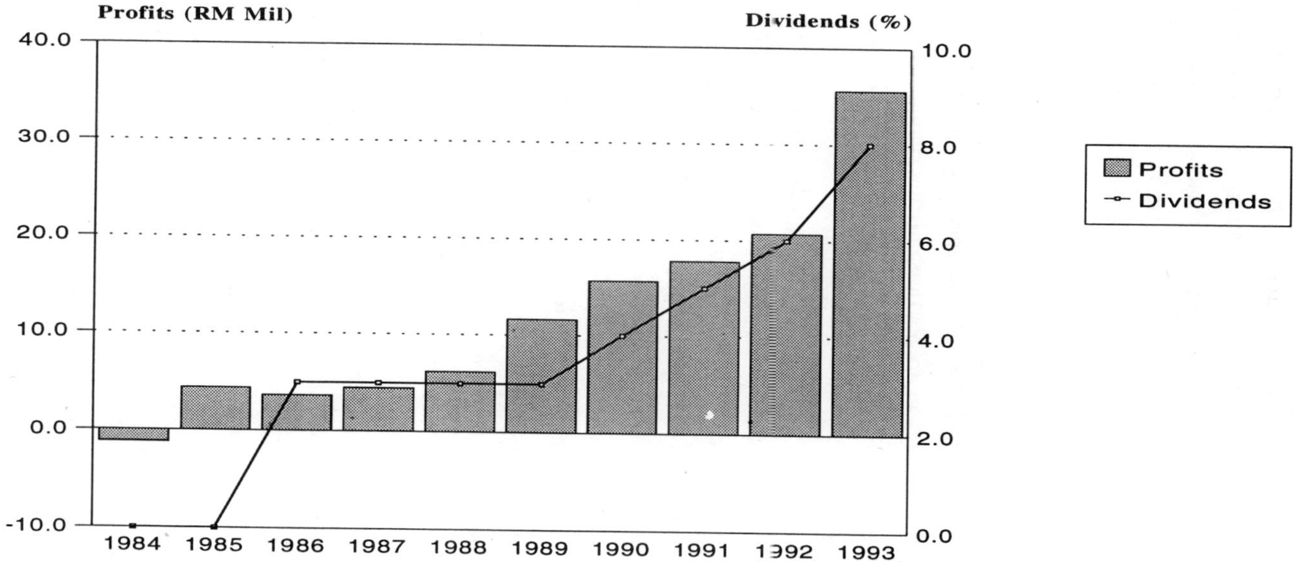

	1984	1985	1986	1987	1988	1989	1990	1991	1992	1993
Profits	-1.2	4.4	3.7	4.5	6.2	11.6	15.7	17.8	20.7	35.6
Dividends	0.0	0.0	3.0	3.0	3.0	3.0	4.0	5.0	6.0	8.0

Sources: BIMB Annual Reports.

insofar as it is returns and not simply Islamic solidarity which attracts depositors, excessive dividend payments may inhibit deposit growth, and hence the long-term value of the shareholders' assets.

Bank Islam Malaysia calculates its returns to depositors and those to shareholders on a different basis. As Figure 6.6 shows, returns to depositors are largely determined by income from the direct financing operations of the bank through *Bai Bithaman Ajil*, *Ijarah*, etc., whereas returns to shareholders are more dependent on the returns from the bank's investments in Islamically acceptable government stocks. Commissions on bank services are also a significant source of shareholder income, whereas these are not taken into account in the calculation of depositor returns.

The reason for this distinct accounting is to keep the returns to depositors closely in line with the returns from the bank's financing, which, of course, often benefits the same depositors. To qualify for financing, a client must first open an account with the bank. The idea is that the bank should act as a true intermediary, the *sahib al mal* (productive financier) in the Islamic sense. The bank is not however acting as a financier for its own shareholders, with whom its relationship is quite different, as they are its owners. Their obligations, and indeed their risks, are much greater than those of the depositors, as in the event of the institution's collapse, the depositors would have first claim on the bank's assets, not the shareholders.

Figure 6.7 shows the shareholding ownership structure of BIMB, with the vertical axis scaled logarithmically to reflect the skewed concentration of ownership. Less than one-quarter per cent of the shareholders own over four-fifths of the bank's shares, but the largest shareholders are institutions, with Menteri Kewangan (Diperbadankan) Malaysia, Jami Company and Lembaga Urusan dan Tabung Haji together owning over 40 per cent of the equity. The bank has been keen, however, to attract private Muslim investors of relatively modest means to give the institution a clear identity and business profile in the Bumiputera community. This is reflected in the shareholdings of between RM500

FIGURE 6.6
Bank Islam Malaysia: Sources of Income

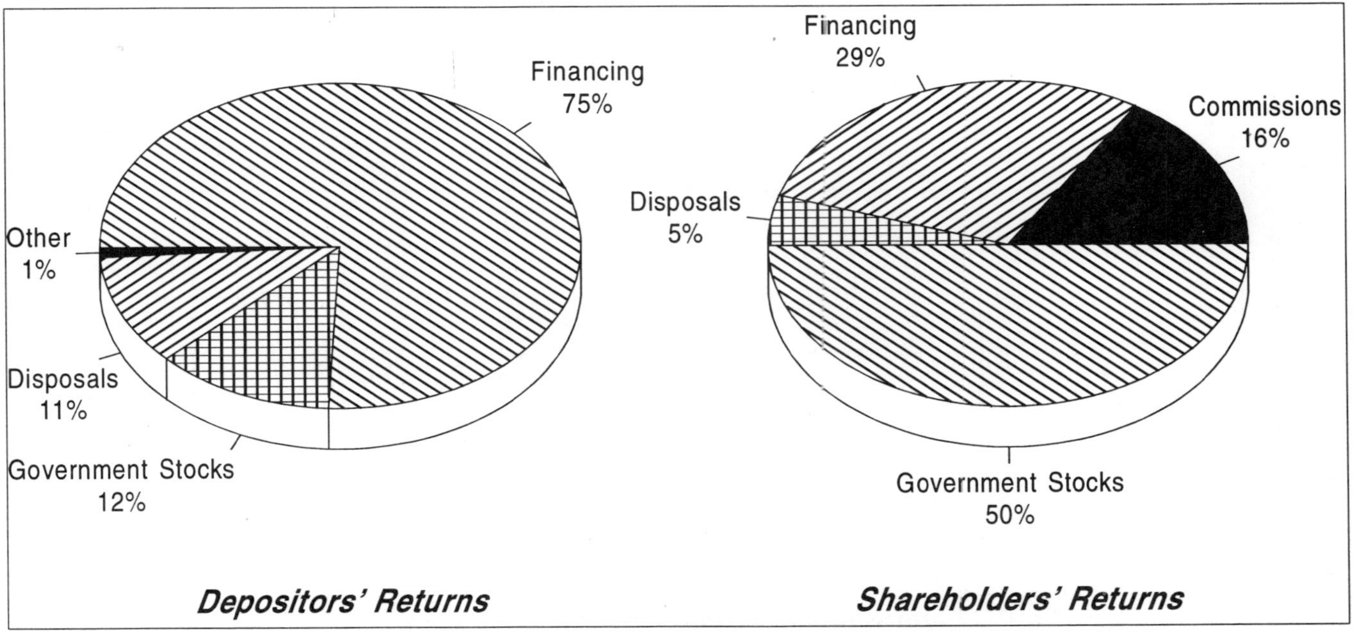

Sources: BIMB Annual Reports.

FIGURE 6.7

Bank Islam Malaysia: Shareholding Structure

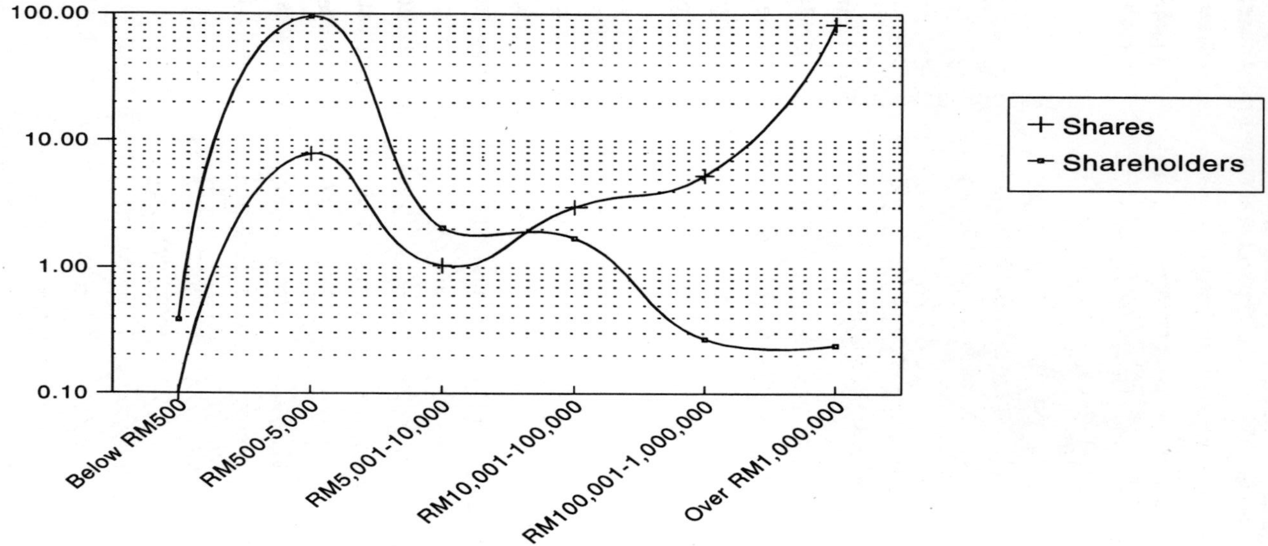

Shares	0.00	7.84	1.04	2.99	5.33	82.80
Shareholders	0.38	95.35	2.05	1.71	0.27	0.24

Sources: BIMB Annual Reports.

and RM5,000 accounting for over 95 per cent of investors. Almost 8,500 shareholders are in this ownership category, which indicates the extent of direct popular participation in BIMB.[12] This participation has clearly increased the profile of the bank, but it still remains very much a minor player in the Malaysian banking scene, existing in its own niche market.

External Islamic Financing

The major external source of Islamic development finance for Malaysia is the Jeddah-based Islamic Development Bank (IDB). This institution provides support for trade and project finance for all Muslim countries, and in many respects functions as a type of world bank for its subscribers.[13] Malaysia was a founding member of the bank in 1974, with an initial subscription of US$16 million. Since then as all the IDB's authorized capital was paid up, Malaysia increased its subscription to US$40.4 million, representing just over 2 per cent of the total paid-up capital of the bank.[14]

Malaysia has not been a major beneficiary of IDB funding, as most trade and project financing has involved Middle Eastern and North African countries, and to a lesser extent, Pakistan and Bangladesh. A total of eight projects have been funded since 1974 (with a combined value of US$53 million), one of the largest of which was an institute for palm-oil seed research.[15] There was also US$42 million advanced for trade finance, most of which was used to cover the additional costs of oil imports after the oil price rises of 1974 and 1979. The Islamic Development Bank is now trying to help the lowest income Muslim states, in addition to its new members amongst the Muslim states of the former Soviet Union. Malaysia remains an active member of IDB, but the possibilities for it receiving substantial development finance from this source are limited, given the bank's funding criteria and priorities.

The prospects for large capital inflows from the OPEC states of the Middle East are now also considerably diminished as a result of the oil price falls, and the debts incurred by the Arabian peninsula states during and following from the Gulf War. Saudi Arabia's official reserves are now much depleted, and the kingdom has been forced to borrow from international financial markets. As a result of mounting budget deficits, its national debt has risen to US$55 billion, the equivalent of 45 per cent of GDP.[16] Other Gulf states are in a similar situation, and although there has been an improvement in the financial position of some Arab states, notably Egypt, countries such as these are recipients of development finance, not providers.

Of greater and long-term significance to Malaysia is the possibility of portfolio investment flows into quoted companies on the Kuala Lumpur Stock Exchange from investment companies and individuals of high net worth in other Muslim countries. The stock exchange in Malaysia is recognized as a significant emerging market for Western portfolio investors, including insurance companies, investment trusts, mutual funds (in the United States) and unit trusts (in the United Kingdom). Although the market has suffered a setback since the beginning of 1994, there is sufficient maturity to maintain the long-term interest of American and European investors. Foreign investment in the Malaysian manufacturing sector amounted to over US$7 billion in 1992 and US$3 billion in 1993, although some of this was direct investment by multinational companies rather than portfolio investment.[17] Nevertheless with a market capitalization of almost US$100 billion, the value of stocks on the KLSE is not far behind those of Seoul, Taipei and Mexico City, and is well above those of Rio, Bombay and Bangkok. The 373 quoted companies means width as well as depth.[18]

One challenge from the viewpoint of Islamic development finance is to harness funds from Muslim investors into the stock market. Equity finance is by nature participatory, and can therefore accord well with the principles of *mudarabah* and *musharakah*. There is of course scope for harnessing funds from the Bumiputera Muslim investors in Malaysia,[19] but the potential for attracting funds from the Muslim countries of the Middle East should not be ignored. The fall in oil prices has had a much greater adverse effect on public than private finances. There are still many companies and individuals of high net worth in Saudi Arabia with surplus funds to place abroad. In the coming decade portfolio investment flows to developing countries are likely to exceed aid and official development assistance. This has already been the case since the late 1980s. Islamic financing has to adjust to these new realities. Institutions such as BIMB have played an important educational role in demonstrating the commercial viability of Islamic finance, but their quantitative effect has been limited. In the long run the major impact of Islamic financing may come through the development of appropriate vehicles for handling equity investment, such as Islamic investment companies and unit trusts. Malaysia has the market, but it has yet to develop the instruments to serve it.

Notes

1 Figures from *World Bank Atlas*, 25th edition, Washington, 1993, p.9 and p.19.

2 *The World in 1994*, Economist Publications, London, p.93.

3 United Nations Human Development Report, New York, 1993, p.135.

4 World Bank, *World Development Report*, Washington, 1993, p.241.

5 Brian Wawn, *The Economies of the ASEAN Countries*, St Martins Press, New York, 1982, pp.40–41.

6 Figures from the IMF data tapes accessed through Datastream, the on-line computer financial economic and financial information service.

7 Figures from World Bank, *World Tables*, Washington, 1993, Tables 13 and 14, pp.50–55.

8 "Islamic Banking Laws of Malaysia," in John Presley (ed.), *Directory of Islamic Financial Institutions*, Croom Helm, 1988, Appendix A, pp.311–328.

9 Paul Gower, *Islamic Banking within the Financial Development of Malaysia*, Durham University M.A. thesis, 1991, p.92.

10 Economic indicators from IMF tapes accessed through Datastream.

11 Ibid.

12 Bank Islam Malaysia Bhd., Annual Report, 1993, Kuala Lumpur, p.65.

13 Rodney Wilson, "The Islamic Development Bank as an Aid Agency for Muslim Countries," *Journal of International Development*, 4 (1), October 1989, pp.444–466.

14 Islamic Development Bank, Annual Report, 1991, Jeddah, p.181.

15 Ibid., p.121 and p.127.

16 Rodney Wilson, "Middle East: Oil Effects," *Oxford Analytica*, January 19, 1994, p.1.

17 Kieran Crooke, "Danger Signals Flash on Malaysia's Road Ahead," *Financial Times*, London, January 17, 1994, p.7.

18 *L'Expansion*, Paris, 462, October 21–November 9, 1993, pp.122–123.

19 Nublan Zaky Yusoff, *An Islamic Perspective of the Stock Market*, Dian Darulnaim Sdn. Bhd., Kuala Lumpur, 1992, pp.1–3.

Chapter 7

Bank Islam Malaysia: Performance Evaluation, 1983–1993

WONG CHOO SUM

THE ESTABLISHMENT OF Bank Islam Malaysia Bhd. (BIMB) in 1983 is the forerunner to the development of an Islamic banking system in Malaysia. The vision for this system took another step towards reality with the recent launching of Phase I of Interest-Free Banking Scheme (IFBS) by three commercial banks on a pilot basis on March 4, 1993 and Phase II with four more phases in the pipeline.

The objective of this chapter is to evaluate the performance of BIMB over the last 10 years of its operation, as BIMB's performance has important implication on the viability of Islamic banking system in Malaysia.

This chapter is divided into two parts. The first part will cover the literature review, research methodology, company's profile and its banking operations. The second half will delve into the evaluation of BIMB's performance.

Literature Review

The establishment of BIMB is regarded a healthy and positive sign towards the development of a dual banking system in Malaysia. The chief aim of Islamic banking is to provide an alternative to the conventional interest-based banking system. Whether BIMB has performed well in the banking industry has been widely debated among professionals and scholars.

Man's evaluated the performance of BIMB from 1984 to 1985 in terms of growth of customers' deposits, total assets, liquidity requirements, investments and its management.[1] He found that the progress made was encouraging and the experience was somewhat similar to those of Islamic bank's in other countries.

Though BIMB may have achieved the conventional banking objectives of profitability and liquidity, it is equally important for it to take into account the desirable goals of an Islamic economy system. For example, the eradication of poverty, optimum utilization of resources, equitable distribution of wealth and income.

In terms of assets and profits, the bank occupied the thirteenth position while in terms of deposits, it ranked tenth among the 23 locally incorporated banks as at December 31, 1982.[2]

A few studies on BIMB have been conducted before its debut on the Kuala Lumpur Stock Exchange (KLSE) on January 17, 1992. Most analysts were satisfied with the performance of BIMB.

Mahidin evaluated BIMB's financial performance over a period of five years (1986–1990)[3] in terms of growth of assets, shareholders' fund, profits, customers' deposits and financing. He concludes that the bank has lived up to its corporate mission of "providing banking and financial facilities which are in compliance with Shariah and at the same time attain viability and growth."

Anwar who evaluated the growth of BIMB's assets, deposits and financing given during the 1985–1990 period claimed its performance to be encouraging.[4] He indicates that the growth rates of deposits imply growing public demand for profit-sharing contracts. He concludes that the financial needs of 53 per cent of the Muslim population in Malaysia were not adequately catered for according to the tenets of Islam as there was only a small number of Islamic financial institutions locally.

Bank Islam Malaysia has been criticized for its heavy reliance on the less risky modes of financing, that is, *Murabaha*, *Bai Bithaman Ajil* and *Ijarah*. To some scholars, these modes of financing which entail fixed profit margins represent "backdoor *riba*". Secondly, its operations are geared towards profit maximization rather than focusing on socio-economic goals such as eradication of poverty.

Abdul Halim, the managing director of BIMB argues that the concept of "backdoor *riba*" is alien to Shariah.[5] In Shariah, if a contract is permissible, it is permissible irrespective of the frequency and the extent of its application. Thus it cannot be a doorway to *riba*.

He further states that the operations of BIMB belongs to the *tijari* (commercial) sector. Therefore, BIMB should operate like a commercial institution. While, the fulfilment of socio-economic objectives should lie with the institutions operating under the *ijtimai* (welfare) sector.[6]

Hussein, the Governor of Bank Negara declared that a "full-fledged" Islamic financial system is very much desired.[7] In particular, proposal allowing the conventional banks to set up their own Islamic counters is under serious considerations.

The recent launching of Phase I of IFBS on March 1993 is the launching pad for the development of an Islamic interbank money market system and capital market system.[8] Currently, more than 20 Islamic banking instruments are being offered under this scheme.

Experiences have shown that Islamic banking system can coexist with conventional banking system and continue to grow and prosper. Therefore, a continued evaluation of BIMB performance is necessary.

Research Methodology

Both primary and secondary data were used in the preparation of this chapter. The primary data was acquired through personal interviews with BIMB's personnel, while the secondary data was obtained from library research. The references that I used are Bank Negara Annual Report, various publications, books, newspaper articles, magazines and BIMB annual reports.

Company's Profile

The Islamic Banking Act 1983 came into effect on March 11, 1983 which modelled on the existing Banking Act 1973. It paved the way for the establishment of banks based on Islamic principles to fill the void in the existing banking system: to meet the banking and credit needs of the Muslim population in Malaysia in accordance to the rules of Shariah which prohibits *riba* (interest).

Bank Islam Malaysia Bhd. was incorporated on March 1983 and commenced operations on July 1, 1983 with a branch in Kuala Lumpur. Subsequently, 28 branches were opened throughout Malaysia, bringing the total number to 29 at the end of December 1991. To date, BIMB has three subsidiaries and 33 branches located mainly in the urban areas throughout Malaysia.

The corporate mission of the bank is to operate as a commercial bank functioning on the basis of Islamic principles, providing banking facilities and services to Muslims and the whole population of this country, with viability and capability to sustain itself and grow in the process.

Its corporate objectives are as follows:

a. To provide its customers with Islamic banking facilities and services of the highest possible quality.
b. To attain viability and sufficient level of profitability to sustain growth.
c. To develop and foster a competent and innovative management imbibed with high standard of integrity and Islamic banking professionalism.
d. To develop a motivated work-force inculcated with the appropriate ethics, fully committed to the bank and providing efficient and courteous service to the customers.
e. To constantly strive to protect its shareholders' interests.
f. To be always conscious of its responsibilities and duties as an Islamic corporate citizen.

The organizational structure of the bank is as depicted in Appendix A (at the end of this chapter). The structure consists of three divisions with line function of operations (trade finance, treasury and corporate investments) and three other divisions with staff functions (establishment, accounts, and legal and secretarial). Each division is divided into departments and further subdivided into units as deemed necessary.

Banking Operation

Bank Islam Malaysia offers all the conventional banking services such as to accept dcposits, granting credit facilities, provision of safe-keeping facilities and fund transfer.

Sources of Fund

- **Current Accounts**
  Wadiah (Guaranteed Custody).
- **Savings Accounts**
  Wadiah (Guaranteed Custody).
- **General Investments Accounts**
  Mudarabah (Trustee Profit Sharing).
- **Special Investments Accounts**
  Mudarabah (Trustee Profit Sharing).

Applications of Fund

- **Equity Financing**
  a. *Mudarabah* (Trustee Profit Sharing); and
  b. *Musharakah* (Joint-Venture Profit Sharing).
- **Term Financing**
  Bai Bithaman Ajil (Deferred Instalment Sale).
- **Trade Financing**
  a. Letters of credit *Wakalah* (Agency);

b. Letters of credit *Murabaha* (Deferred Lump Sum Sale);
c. Letters of credit *Musharakah* (Joint-Venture Profit Sharing);
d. *Murabaha* Working Capital Financing (Deferred Lump-Sum Sale);
e. Islamic Accepted Bill;
f. Islamic Credit Refinancing;
g. Investment; and
h. *Musharakah* (Joint-Venture Profit Sharing).

Performance Evaluation

In this exercise, BIMB's performance will be evaluated based on a few parameters. Firstly, in terms of the growth of its deposits and total assets. Secondly, on its profits and the returns to its depositors and shareholders. Thirdly, its modes of financing and usage of funds. And finally, on how it discharges its social obligation as an Islamic bank.

TABLE 7.1
Bank Islam Malaysia:
Sources of Funds (RM Mil) and Annual Growth (%)

Year	1984	1985	1986	1987	1988	1989	1990	1991
No. of Branches	4	8	14	18	21	24	27	29
Current Accounts	40.0 –	43.2 8%	56.6 31%	123.0 117%	142.3 15.7%	140.6 -1.2%	197.4 40.4%	220.4 11.7%
Savings Accounts	26.1 –	46.5 78%	78.2 68.2%	113.8 45.5%	152.8 34.3%	181.5 18.8%	212.7 17.2%	249.5 17.3%
General Investments	101.2 –	276.2 173%	404.2 46.3%	572.1 41.4%	274.6 26.7%	943.9 30.3%	725.1 -23%	609.2 -16%
Special Investments	71.0 –	49.4 -30%	36.8 -26%	16.8 -54%	23.4 39.3%	5.5 -77%	123.5 2146%	96.0 -22%
TOTAL	238.3 –	415.3 74.3%	575.8 38.6%	325.7 43%	1,043.1 26.3%	1,272 21.9%	1,258.7 -1%	1,175 -6.6%

Sources: BIMB Annual Reports, 1984–1991.

Growth of Deposits

The number of depositors have increased during the 1984–1991 period whereas the growth of deposits has declined from 74.3 per cent in 1985 to 26.3 per cent in 1988 and slipped further to -6.6 per cent in 1991 (Table 7.1).

Compared to the industry, the industry's performance declined from 13.7 per cent in 1989 to 3.7 per cent in 1990 but increased back to 22.4 per cent in 1991 (Table 7.2); while BIMB's performance declined from 21.9 per cent to -1 per cent and -6.6 per cent over the same period. It was therefore expanding at a faster rate in the beginning and slowed down in the later years. The liberalization of the Base Lending Rate has partly contributed to the decrease in the growth of deposits. When conventional banks are free to set the rate of return to deposits, the higher rate of return offered by them may resulted in some switching of BIMB's depositors who are primarily interested in higher rate of return.

TABLE 7.2
Commercial Banks:
Financial Performance (RM Mil) and Annual Growth (%)

Year	1989	1990	1991
Assets	112,614.8 21.06%	129,197.0 14.7%	151,967.5 17.62%
Financing	67,141.5 18.19%	80,762.7 20.29%	98,541.3 22.01%
Deposits*	59,882.5 13.7%	62,259.1 3.97%	76,242.9 22.46%

* Excluding NCDs, NIF deposits and special deposits.
Sources: The Association of Banks in Malaysia, Annual Reports, 1989–1991.

During the 1984–1991 period, the rate of return on 12-month deposits with BIMB were lower than those of conventional banks as shown in Table 7.3. To compete in the banking industry, BIMB must be able to give a return that is at least equivalent to that which is offered in the industry.

TABLE 7.3
Rates of Return on 12-Month Deposits (%)

Year	Commercial Banks	Bank Islam Malaysia
1984	10.80	6.95
1985	7.50	7.64
1986	7.00	6.60
1987	4.25	5.88
1988	4.25	4.54
1989	5.50	4.64
1990	7.25	4.72
1991*	7.00	5.36

* As of May 1991.
Sources: Bank Negara, *Quarterly Bulletin*, January–March 1991; *Money and Banking in Malaysia, 1959–1989*, Bank Negara Malaysia.

Table 7.4 indicates that there is a positive correlation between the growth of depositors and the rate of return. For example, the rate of return for BIMB 12-month deposits which was 7.64 per cent in 1985 decreased to 4.72 per cent in 1990, but increased back to 5.36 per cent in 1991. We also see the same growth pattern in the annual growth rate of the number of depositors for General Investment Accounts. At 89 per cent in 1985 to -2.8 per cent in 1990 and increased to 8.1 per cent in 1990. Therefore, we could see that the growth of deposits is highly influenced by the rate of return.

Total Assets

During 1984–1991, the total assets of BIMB increased from RM326 million in 1984 to RM1,357 million in 1991, representing an increase of

316 per cent (Table 7.5). But the annual growth rates were on a decline except in 1987, from 58 per cent in 1985 to 19 per cent in 1989 and -3 per cent in 1991. This pattern of unusually high initial growth and subsequent decline in the later years is also experienced by most Islamic banks worldwide.[9]

TABLE 7.4
Annual Growth Rates of Depositors (%)

Year	Annual Growth of Depositors of General Investment Accounts	Rates of Return on 12-Month Deposits
1984	–	6.95
1985	89.0	7.64
1986	42.7	6.60
1987	15.7	5.88
1988	36.8	4.54
1989	-1.3	4.64
1990	-2.8	4.72
1991	8.1	5.36

Sources: BIMB Annual Reports, 1984–1991.

In Malaysia, the total assets of commercial banks had declined from 21.06 per cent in 1989 to 14.70 per cent in 1990 but increased to 17.62 per cent in 1991 (Table 7.2). This indicates that while the growth trend of the banking industry had moderated in the late 1980s, BIMB's trend is still showing a decline.

Returns to Shareholders

The shareholders' funds have been increasing at an average rate of 3.5 per cent during the 1985–1991 period (Table 7.5). In terms of the shareholders' fund, BIMB is ranked twelfth.[10]

Dividends are paid to shareholders after making provision for taxes, *zakat* and statutory reserve funds. Table 7.6 shows that BIMB's dividend payment during the 1988–1991 period can be considered low in contrast to those paid by Malayan Banking Bhd. and Public Bank Bhd.

TABLE 7.5
Bank Islam Malaysia:
Financial Performance (RM Mil) and Annual Growth (%)

Year	1984	1985	1986	1987	1988	1989	1990	1991
Assets*	326.0 –	514.0 58.0%	683.0 33.0%	932.0 37.0%	1,153.0 24.0%	1,368.0 19.0%	1,396.0 2.0%	1,357.0 -3.0%
Shareholders' Funds	78.1 –	80.6 3.2%	82.9 2.9%	83.8 1.1%	85.8 2.4%	89.4 4.2%	92.4 3.4%	99.4 7.6%
Profits**	-1.3 –	4.4 –	3.7 -16.0%	4.5 22.0%	6.2 38.0%	10.0 61.0%	13.4 34.0%	14.1 5.2%
Deposits	241.4 –	410.2 70.0%	566.9 38.2%	809.1 42.7%	1,022.0 26.3%	1,229.0 20.3%	1,220.0 -0.7%	1,175.0 -3.8%
Financing***	161.6 –	322.0 99.8%	395.3 23.0%	428.6 8.4%	609.4 42.2%	666.1 9.3%	807.8 21.3%	789.3 -2.2%

* Assets before contra items.
** Profits before *zakat* and taxes.
*** Total amount of financing less provision for bad debts.
Sources: BIMB Annual Reports, 1984–1991.

At the time of BIMB's debut in the KLSE on January 17, 1992 Inter-Pacific Securities (IPS) recommended investors to buy BIMB's shares at RM2.20 per share by placing the counter on a prospective price-earning ratio of 23 times for the fiscal year 1992. IPS indicated that BIMB was in a sound position with a capital adequacy of 20 per cent—substantially higher than the industry's average.[11]

Profit before Taxes and Zakat

Bank Islam Malaysia recorded a loss of RM1.3 million in 1984 due to high initial operating costs. But it only took about 18 months to break-even. Profits were generated in 1985 at RM4.4 million and increased to

RM14.1 million in 1991, representing an increase of 220 per cent over the period of 8 years (1984–1991).

TABLE 7.6
Rates of Dividends Paid to Shareholders (%)

Year / Bank	1988	1989	1990	1991
BIMB	2.0	3.0	4.0	5.0
Malayan Banking	6.5	10.0	9.0	n.a.
Public Bank	6.0	6.0	6.0	n.a.

Sources: BIMB Annual Reports, 1984–1991; Malayan Banking Annual Reports, 1988–1990; Public Bank Annual Reports, 1988–1990.

In terms of pre-tax profits, BIMB ranked thirteenth which is considered a "middle position" in the banking industry.[12] BIMB pays *zakat* over and above the normal corporate tax, amounting to approximately RM500,000.00 every year.

TABLE 7.7
Bank Islam Malaysia:
Overall Performance, 1984–1991

Year / Ratio	1984	1985	1986	1987	1988	1989	1990	1991
P/A	-0.004	0.009	0.005	0.005	0.005	0.007	0.009	0.010
P/SF	-0.017	0.050	0.040	0.050	0.070	0.110	0.150	0.140
P/D	-0.005	0.010	0.006	0.006	0.006	0.008	0.100	0.010
P/F	0.008	0.010	0.009	0.010	0.010	0.020	0.020	0.020

P/A (Profits to Assets); P/SF (Profits to Shareholders' Funds); P/D (Profits to Deposits); P/F (Profits to Financing).
Sources: BIMB Annual Reports, 1984–1991.

To examine the overall business performance of BIMB, the ratio of profits to assets, to shareholders' funds, to deposits and to financing are calculated (Table 7.7). The negative ratios in 1984 signifies a negative return in the first year of operation. Over the period of 8 years the performance of BIMB has improved although the growth of its profit from the utilizations of its assets, shareholders' funds, deposits, and its financing is not significant enough.

The trend in the low growth of its profits warrants immediate attention to increase the effectiveness and efficiency in the managing of its funds and assets. Suggestions have come from certain quarters that BIMB should go into long-term investments (that is, partnership and project financing) that could generate higher returns even though the risks are much greater.

Modes of Financing

Bank Islam Malaysia's modes of financing will give us a picture how well BIMB has utilized its resources to generate revenues. Its five most important modes of financing are *Bai Bithaman Ajil*, *Murabaha*, *Ijarah*, *Mudarabah* and *Musharakah*.

Bai Bithaman Ajil claimed the highest share of total financing. It increased from 49.1 per cent in 1984 to 78.7 per cent in 1987 and decreased slightly to 73.7 per cent in 1991 (Table 7.8). This is followed by *murabaha*, although it had declined from 37.2 per cent to 15.0 per cent, that is, by 13.2 per cent over the same period.

Bai Bithaman Ajil and *murabaha* are similar in terms of its operations with the exception that the former recognizes payments in installments. These modes of financing are criticized because of the resemblance of their profit margins to interest. Some Islamic bankers agreed that *Bai Bithaman Ajil* and *murabaha* should be phased out and be replaced by other financial instruments which are more equitable to both the borrowers and the lenders.[13]

Chapra argues that *murabaha* is an easy way out for Islamic banks interested in abolishing *riba*, but it puts the entire risk of financing onto the borrower.[14] Therefore, this mode of financing should be played down in favour of other modes of financing.

TABLE 7.8
Bank Islam Malaysia Bank:
Modes of Financing (% to Total Financing)

Year	1984	1985	1986	1987	1988	1989	1990	1991
BBA	49.1	68.4	77.0	78.7	76.0	75.8	70.8	73.7
Murabaha	37.2	22.8	15.5	15.0	18.9	20.9	17.8	13.2
Ijarah	9.3	5.9	4.9	3.4	2.9	3.1	11.2	13.0
Mudarabah	3.1	0.9	0.3	0.3	0.3	0.06	0.04	0.04
Musharakah	1.2	2.0	2.2	2.1	1.8	0.01	0.01	0.01
QH	0.1	–	0.1	0.5	0.4	0.06	0.07	0.07
TOTAL (%)	100	100	100	100	100	100	100	100

BBA (*Bai-Bithaman Ajil*); QH (*Qard al-Hasanah*).
Sources: BIMB Annual Reports, 1984–1991.

Ghamdi of Al-Rajhi Banking Corporation in Saudi Arabia argued that the present emphasis on *murabaha* could be allowed but shall be phased out once Islamic bankings evolves into a much bigger and developed system.

During the 1984–1991 period, *ijarah* (leasing) became more significant in the later years. Starting at 9.3 per cent in 1984, it decreased drastically to 2.9 per cent in 1988 but increased significantly to 13.0 per cent in 1991.

Nienhaus proposed that to reduce short-term financing,15 corporate financing could be done under non-participation arrangements like leasing.

Mudarabah financing represents less than 1 per cent throughout the 1985–1991 period with only once at 3.1 per cent in 1984. Similarly, *musharakah* financing was at 1.2 per cent in 1984 to 2.2 per cent in 1986 and since then declined to 0.01 per cent in 1991.

These modes of financing are not popular because of the following reasons:

a. There is a lack of honest and trustworthy entrepreneurs: BIMB had been cheated by some of its customers in the past. Some of them did not declare their profits while others did not possess the skill to participate in business.

b. Bank Islam Malaysia being a commercial bank has to cater to all sorts of financing needs. It is not possible to finance all the needs on the basis of *mudarabah* and *musharakah*.

c. The government also provides procedures for the bank to undertake certain projects on the basis of equity financing. As some of these procedures are not in line with Shariah, the bank has to forgo those projects.[16]

d. There is a lack of medium- and long-term funds which is one the conditions for *mudarabah* and *musharakah* financings. The major portion of BIMB's funds are in the short term with the remainder at best in the medium term.

   The deposits in current and savings accounts are by the dictate of *Wadiah* contract subject to withdrawal by the depositors, either partially or wholly on demand. Whereas, the deposits in investment accounts are normally for periods of 24 months and below. Therefore, a solid fund that can be used in *mudarabah* and *musharakah* has yet to be created.

e. Long-term financings involve higher risks and there is a lack of qualified personnel to undertake the operations. Therefore, BIMB is partial towards short-term investment financing. To overcome this problem, Al-Harran has suggested the setting up of an Islamic investment company and an Islamic consultancy house.[17] These companies will first identify the potential sectors such as the manufacturing, constructions, services and small- and medium-sized industries. They will then evaluate the individual project based on its economic and financial viability and propose it to the bank for funding.

The recent development of the IFBS will make it viable to set up another money market and capital market that can fulfil the requirements of Shariah. This will then ensure the provision of funds for long-term projects such as project financing.

Usage of Funds

A review of BIMB's usage of funds will indicate to what extent BIMB has contributed to the development of various sectors in the economy. During the period of 1984 to 1991, the manufacturing sector had received the largest share at 5.1 per cent in 1984 to 19.5 per cent in 1988 and 30.3 per cent in 1991 (Table 7.9).

This is followed by the real estate sector which increased from 1.4 per cent in 1984 to 25.4 per cent in 1988 but declined to 10.1 per cent in 1990. While, on the other extreme, the mining and quarrying and the agricultural sectors benefited little from BIMB's financing. The agricultural sector which received 0.5 per cent in 1984 received an increased to 5.2 per cent in 1988 and remained stagnant at 5.2 per cent in 1991. While the mining and quarrying sector received 8.5 per cent in 1984 but declined to 2.4 per cent in 1984 and negligible in 1991.

This indicates that BIMB financing is mainly focusing on the manufacturing, wholesale, retail and trade sectors and little on the agricultural and the mining and quarrying sectors. This reflects the structural transformation of the Malaysian economy from one which is agricultural based to one which is based on an agricultural and manufacturing mix. This trend is basically similar with those of other commercial banks.

Social Obligation

The bank discharges its social obligation through *qard al-hasanah* and *zakat* contribution. *Qard al-hasanah* is providing loans to those deserving customers without any charges. However, this portion of financing is insignificant at only 0.07 per cent in 1991 (Table 7.8).

Thus BIMB has been accused of concentrating on profit maximization, while neglecting its welfare-oriented operations.[18]

TABLE 7.9
Bank Islam Malaysia and Commercial Banks: Sectoral Distribution of Financing (%)

Year	1984	1985	1986	1987	1988	1989	1990	1991
Agriculture	0.5 (6.1)	3.3 (6.0)	24 (6.1)	3.7 (6.0)	5.2 (5.4)	5.2 (5.4)	5.3 (5.2)	5.2 (4.8)
Mining & Quarrying	8.5 (1.1)	4.0 (1.0)	3.0 (0.8)	3.9 (0.8)	2.4 (1.4)	– (1.3)	– (1.0)	– (0.9)
Manu-facturing	-5.1 (18.1)	3.8 (17.5)	13.6 (17.1)	12.0 (17.5)	19.5 (19.7)	28.4 (20.9)	34.2 (23.2)	30.3 (24.2)
W/sale & Retail Trade	25.1 (18.7)	28.3 (17.9)	16.5 (17.4)	15.5 (17.3)	11.9 (16.9)	6.8 (15.7)	5.9 (14.4)	6.2 (13.2)
Transport & Storage	4.7 (1.8)	4.5 (1.6)	4.6 (1.4)	4.2 (1.3)	5.5 (1.5)	4.5 (1.9)	3.4 (1.7)	3.0 (2.0)
Business Services	4.9 (12.0)	13.8 (11.9)	14.5 (11.6)	18.4 (10.9)	3.8 (10.2)	4.1 (11.0)	3.8 (11.3)	4.0 (11.8)
Real Estate	1.4 (13.8)	2.9 (14.2)	5.8 (14.3)	10.7 (14.8)	25.4 (14.1)	18.7 (12.7)	14.2 (11.3)	10.1 (10.1)
Misc. incl. Housing	43.9 (20.7)	34.1 (22.3)	34.5 (23.6)	25.6 (23.5)	25.0 (23.4)	25.1 (23.9)	26.8 (25.1)	33.1 (26.0)
TOTAL (%)	100	100	100	100	100	100	100	100

Figures represent percentage share of total financing for BIMB. Figures in parentheses represent share of total financing for commercial banks.
Sources: BIMB Annual Reports, 1984–1991; Bank Negara Monthly Statistics Bulletin, April 1992, p.22.

The Managing Director of BIMB argues that BIMB belonged to the *tijari* (commercial) sector of the economy. Thus, its main task is to operate profitably within the framework of Shariah principles. As for equitable distribution of income is concerned, like collecting *zakat* and *sadaqah*, he claims that it is primarily the responsibility of the *siasi* (government) and *ijtimai* (welfare) sectors of the economy.

With regard to *zakat* contribution, BIMB has been paying *zakat* since its inception in 1984. *Zakat* is meant to redistribute the wealth and income of the rich to help the poor. Its *zakat* contribution has ranged from RM358,000 (1988) to RM663,000 (1991), depending on the profitability of its operations (Table 7.10). Over the years, BIMB's *zakat* contribution has increased in proportion to its profits.

TABLE 7.10
Bank Islam Malaysia:
***Zakat* Contribution**

Year	Amount (RM'000)
1984	484
1985	415
1986	377
1987	381
1988	358
1989	467
1990	449
1991	663

Sources: BIMB Annual Reports, 1984–1991.

Conclusion

For a bank that has only been operating for ten years, BIMB's achievements is commendable, although there are shortcomings in its modes of financing. Because the underlying spirit of Islamic banking is to abolish the inequity which arises due to the practice of *riba* (interest), where all the risks are borne by the borrower, the concept of profit and loss sharing was introduced to ensure that both the lender and the borrower would bear the risks. Since BIMB is partial towards short-term financing, it has failed to uphold this fundamental spirit of an Islamic bank.

Nevertheless, it has proven that an Islamic bank has the ability to maintain its viability and growth in a capitalistic financial environment. It has also created the awareness of a possible alternative to the conventional interest-based banking system. One way or another, it has contributed to the setting up of the Islamic counters in the conventional banks.

Generally, BIMB has not made enough significant contribution in achieving the equitable distribution of income in Malaysia, it has played its role in helping to achieve the socio-economic objectives of an Islamic economy through *qard al-hasanah* and *zakat* contribution. And much work still need to be done as the gap between the rich and the poor is widening, where there is a great difference between the standard of living of those in the urban and the rural areas.

Therefore, there is a need for a continuous evaluation on BIMB in the future as the banking environment becoming more dynamic with the infusion of the Islamic banking system.

Notes

1 Zakaria Man, "Islamic Banking: The Malaysian Experience," in M. Ariff (ed.), *Islamic Banking in Southeast Asia*, Institute of Southeast Asian Studies, Singapore, 1988, pp.67–99.

2 Kuala Lumpur Bankers Directory 1990/1991, Arab Malaysian Merchant Bank Bhd., p.4.

3 Azzah Mahidin, "Against the Odds," *Malaysian Business*, June 1–15, 1991, pp.9–10 and January 16–31, 1992, pp.73–74.

4 Muhammad Anwar, "The Role of Islamic Financial Institutions in the Socio-Economic Development in Malaysia," *Pakistan Economic Review*, 1991, pp.1,131–1,138.

5 Abdul Halim Ismail, "Shariah and Islamic Economics: Permissibility of Uses of Funds Contract," International Seminar on Islamic Economics, Kuala Lumpur, July 1987, pp.2–5.

6 Id., "Islamic Banking in Malaysia: Some Issues, Problems and Prospects," Seminar on Issues in Islamic Economics, Kuala Lumpur, December 1985, pp.1–3.

7 *Malaysian Business*, January 16–31, 1992, pp.73–74.

8 Kartini Abdul Kadir, *Business Times*, August 23, 1993, p.1.

9 Awsaf Ahmad, *Development and Problems of Islamic Banks*, International Research and Training Institute, Jeddah, 1986, p.38.

10 Kuala Lumpur Bankers Directory 1990/1991, Arab Malaysian Merchant Bank Bhd.

11 *New Straits Times*, January 14, 1992.

12 Azzah Mahidin, op. cit., p.10.

13 *New Straits Times*, January 31, 1992, p.14.

14 Mohammed Al-Ghamdi and M. Umer Chapra expressed these views in a panel discussion on "Development Financing: Experience of Islamic Financial Institutions," Third International Conference on Islamic Economics, Kuala Lumpur, January 27–30, 1992.

15 Volker Nienhaus, "The Performance of Islamic Banks: Trends and Cases," in Chibli Mallat (ed.), *Islamic Law and Finance*, Graham & Trotham, London, 1988.

16 The details of the procedure by the Government is not available because it is considered confidential between BIMB and the Government.

17 Saad Al-Harran, "Time for Long-term Financing," *New Straits Times*, September 11, 1993, p.9.

18 Zakaria Man, "The Prospects for *Mudarabah* and *Musharakah* Financing," International Seminar on Islamic Economics, Kuala Lumpur, 1987, p.22.

Appendix A

Bank Islam Malaysia: Organization Chart

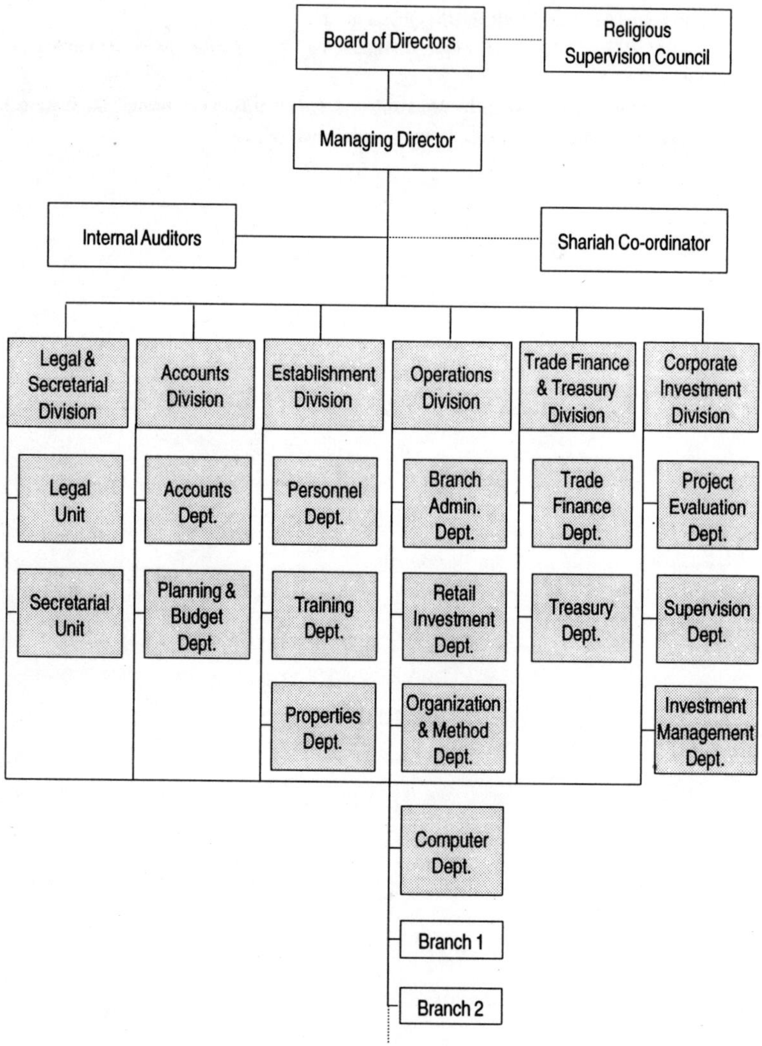

Sources: BIMB

Chapter 8

Bank Islam Malaysia: Market Implications

RADIAH ABDUL KADER

THE SIGNIFICANCE OF Muslim individuals as the target market segment for Islamic banking in Malaysia cannot be underestimated. Their continuous support is essential to ensure the survival of any institution set up specifically to meet their religious obligations and needs. The stagnation of Bank Islam Malaysia's total deposits in 1990 and 1991 is an indication that Islamic banks cannot depend on the corporate sector for deposits when interest rates are rising. It is hence timely for Bank Islam Malaysia Bhd. (BIMB) to devote more of its marketing resources to the retail segment of the market. From the outset, market research is essential to obtain information on the banking needs of the individual customer.

The market for Islamic banking in Malaysia has now become competitive. With the end of BIMB's ten-year protected monopoly in April 1993, an increasing number of conventional banks have begun introducing Islamic counters to capture the Muslim market, which means BIMB can no longer depend on the religious factor to attract deposits. Since the individual customer now has an option between a full-fledged Islamic bank and an Islamic counter it is imperative for BIMB to change its management outlook. Thus to gain a competitive advantage over the other banks, the team at BIMB has to become more aggressive in its marketing approach, more knowledgeable of its existing and potential customers and more skilful in marketing its services.

This chapter is an attempt to examine the Muslim market for BIMB and derive some implications which may be useful to both BIMB and policymakers. It has been designed to understand why, in a country whose population is predominantly Muslim (53 per cent), BIMB has only captured a very small share of deposits; that after ten years (1983–1993) in existence, only about 2 per cent of total commercial bank deposits were held in BIMB. It raises the question of whether Malaysian Muslims are not depositing in the banking system at all or they desire banking services but are not primarily motivated to bank with BIMB.

In general the Muslim market consists of three major segments:

a. The strict or pious Muslims who totally avoid the *riba* banks;
b. The less strict Muslims who hold accounts both at BIMB and interest-based banks; and
c. The least strict Muslims who only patronize conventional banks.

The banking behaviour of these groups differ in many ways. An understanding of their differences may provide some useful information for BIMB in terms of market segmentation so that different products can be targeted for different groups of bank customers.

Our main objectives are, firstly, to examine the banking behaviour of the different categories of BIMB customers and determine the factors that have influenced them to bank at BIMB. Secondly, to examine the perception of the Muslim non-depositors towards BIMB, to find out why conventional banks were more preferred and to identify the main reasons which had discouraged them from opening accounts at BIMB. Finally, some conclusions will be derived in terms of the market implications for BIMB.

Methodology

A survey of the Muslim depositors of BIMB and those of conventional banks was conducted in 1991 as part of a bigger study on Islamic banking in Malaysia which has been reported elsewhere.[1] The respondents comprised the depositors of BIMB and interest-based banks. Because the establishment of BIMB was to cater for the banking needs of Muslims the respondents were confined to Muslims only. It was not feasible to sample rural Muslims since all BIMB branches were concentrated in the urban areas.

Due to several constraints, the survey was confined to the Kuala Lumpur area. The BIMB sample was drawn from the bank's first branch situated at Jalan Raja Laut; while the conventional bank depositors were selected from the branches of the top four domestic commercial banks[2] in the same area. The close proximity of the BIMB branch and the other conventional bank branches assured the existence of a competitive environment whereby the conventional bank depositors were most likely to be aware of the existence of BIMB in the area and had the feasible option of selecting BIMB as their alternative bank. Similarly, the conventional banks were easily accessible to the depositors of BIMB, giving them the same opportunity of transferring their accounts to the interest-based banks if desired.

A total of 380 Muslim depositors were randomly sampled,[3] of which 210 were BIMB depositors being sampled for a period of two weeks. The remaining 170 cases were sampled from the four conventional banks. The smaller sample size was mainly due to the relatively shorter timeframe of one week granted by two of the selected conventional bank.

Analysis of BIMB Depositors

The success of BIMB in providing an Islamic alternative to Western banking would be reflected by its ability to attract depositors to bank exclusively with it. If a majority of depositors bank only with BIMB this implies that it has exerted a great impact on mobilizing savings without interest. Man,[4] however envisaged that a majority of depositors would not bank exclusively with BIMB and still maintain contacts with conventional banks.

The survey finding in Table 8.1 seems to agree with Man's viewpoint: it shows that 61.4 per cent (129) of BIMB depositors had accounts in other banks and only 38.6 per cent (81) bank exclusively at BIMB. The result implies that a majority of depositors do not typically regard BIMB an alternative but rather a complement to conventional banks.

TABLE 8.1
Frequency Distribution of BIMB Depositors

Accounts in Other Banks?	Frequency	%	Cumulative %
Yes	129	61.4	61.4
No	81	38.6	100.0
TOTAL	210	100.0	–

Sources: Survey Finding.

It also interesting to note that among depositors who bank exclusively with the Islamic bank, only about one-third were found to be newcomers into the financial system. More than two-thirds (67.9 per cent) had accounts in conventional banks previously (Table 8.2).

TABLE 8.2
Survey of Conventional Bank Account Holders

Saved in Commercial Banks Before?	Frequency	%	Cumulative %
Yes	55	67.9	67.9
No	26	32.1	100.0
TOTAL	81	100.0	–

Sources: Survey Finding.

To some extent this finding seems to indicate that Malaysian Muslims in urban areas have developed the banking habit and are therefore likely to have kept their money in traditional banks before the establishment of BIMB. This leads to an important implication for the market; that the establishment of BIMB branches in the urban areas has only effected a transfer of resources within the market with little impact on mobilizing new deposits which the interest-based banks might have failed to attract previously because of *riba*. It is therefore not surprising that even after ten years in the market the market share of BIMB in deposit mobilization accounted for less than 2 per cent of total domestic commercial bank deposits.[5] It is envisaged that potential new deposits for BIMB can be mobilized more from the rural areas where a sizeable portion of savings are being hoarded because of the absence of *halal* outlets. The findings of Professor Ungku Aziz in the late 1950s[6] had shown that Muslims in the rural areas were highly pious and had preferred to hoard their savings rather than save in the interest-based banks. It would be of great interest to find out if such behaviour persists today and test the impact of Islamic banking on the mobilization of these rural savings. However, as mentioned earlier, it is not possible to carry out such an investigation within the scope of this study because the present network of BIMB branches are concentrated in the urban areas.

It is also found that deposits were made in conventional banks before the establishment of BIMB for purposes other than the rate of interest. About 20 per cent of the responses indicated that in the absence of an Islamic bank they had no other alternative but to keep their money in conventional banks; 11.9 per cent indicated that their salaries were credited directly into commercial banks; and another 9 per cent trusted the banks for the safety of their money. All three reasons seem to indicate one common purpose among the depositors: to ensure the safety of their money. This further supports the argument that urban Muslims had already developed the banking habit before the establishment of BIMB.

The second category of BIMB depositors are those who also hold accounts in conventional banks. As more than half (61.4 per cent) of the sampled population belonged to this group, it raises the question of the type of accounts held and the reason for opening these accounts. Man[7] believes that these depositors would hold current account in conventional banks, presumably for transactional purposes only as these accounts do not yield any interest.

Our research, however, shows that only a few of these depositors had current accounts in conventional banks, with a majority of accounts in the form of savings (79 per cent). Only 13.2 per cent had current accounts and an insignificant 2.3 per cent made fixed deposits.

The high proportion of savings account held may be explained by the fact they were relatively easy to open: anybody can open a savings account with a deposit as little as RM1, in contrast to the current account which requires an introducer and a minimum deposit of RM500.

TABLE 8.3
Frequency Distribution:
Reasons for Deposits in Other Banks

Reasons	Frequency	%	Cumulative (%)
1. Many Branches	87	22.5	22.5
2. ATM Available	82	21.2	43.7
3. Near Home	43	11.1	54.8
4. Near Workplace	40	10.4	65.2
5. Near to Where I Shop	31	8.0	73.2
6. Well Known	23	6.0	79.2
7. Fast and Efficient Service	16	4.1	83.2
8. Salary Paid There	16	4.1	87.3
9. Higher Interest Rates	4	1.0	88.3
(Gives Only One Reason)	45	11.6	100.0
TOTAL	387*	100.0	–

* Refers to responses, not cases since respondents were asked to give three main reasons (i.e. 3 reasons x 129 cases).
Sources: Survey Finding.

In relation to the high proportion of savings accounts held is the question whether this group of depositors are after all attracted by the relatively higher rates of interest offered on these deposits.

It is evident in Table 8.3 that only 1 per cent of the responses were motivated by the rate of return factor. Conversely, a greater percentage of responses show the importance of factors related to convenience, namely, the number of bank branches (22.5 per cent), the availability of automated teller machines (ATMs) (21.2 per cent) and locational convenience. Apparently these are the three factors that BIMB lacks at its present stage of development. However, other things being equal, this group of depositors are likely to transfer all their accounts to BIMB if these facilities were made available in future.

Nevertheless, our findings seem to suggest that accounts held in the conventional banks were mainly supplementary accounts. Bank Islam Malaysia was typically the primary bank for these depositors because 72 per cent of them had more savings in BIMB than in conventional banks and 58 per cent did more business or had more transactions at BIMB than at conventional banks.

Selection Criteria of BIMB Depositors

The findings in the preceding sections seems to suggest that BIMB individual depositors are generally not concerned with the rates of return on their savings. However, there seems to be some trade-off between religious motivation and convenience, as reflected by the high proportion of accounts still held in conventional banks. Which of these two factors is the stronger motivation would bear some important implications on the marketing strategy of BIMB.

In our analysis, a list of 14 variables which were likely to have influenced depositors' decision to choose BIMB as their primary bank was factor analysed. Since factors such as "religious motivation" and "convenience" are not single measurable entities but are actually the constructs of a number of other directly observable variables,[8] through factor analysis these observable variables can be clustered into smaller sets of factors, in accordance to the underlying property (such as convenience) commonly shared by each group of variables.

The product of the factor analysis as shown in Table 8.4,[9] revealed four factors or criteria on which depositors have based their decisions. These factors may be identified in their order of importance:

Factor 1: Being an Islamic Bank;
Factor 2: Convenient Location;
Factor 3: Loan Opportunity; and
Factor 4: Social Influence.

The "Being an Islamic Bank" factor was thought most appropriate for Factor 1 because all the variables which clustered under this factor (Table 8.4) constituted elements which were unique to the Islamic bank. Variables 1 to 4, namely, "profits paid on savings" (PRSAV), "no interest on savings" (NORIB), "profit-sharing investment" (PLSINV) and "no interest on loans" (LNORIB) differentiate an Islamic bank from its conventional counterpart. The suitability of the factor label is further supported by the fifth variable, "runs on Islamic principles" (ISLM), which generalizes the overall Islamic characteristic of the bank. Since Factor 1 has the highest eigenvalue and variance (3.88 and 27.7 per cent respectively) this necessarily implies that it is the most important factor that has influenced depositors' preference for BIMB.

However, not all depositors were homogeneously influenced by the five variables under Factor 1. Table 8.5 reveals that 94.3 per cent of the depositors have been strongly influenced by the knowledge that the operation of BIMB was on Islamic principles. This high response may be attributed to the increasing awareness of Malaysian Muslims of their religion since the outbreak of the Islamic resurgence in the late 1970s. The establishment of BIMB therefore provides a welcomed opportunity for them to express their faith in the economic field. For these Muslims it is important to ensure that the operations of BIMB is Islamically genuine and legitimate from the Shariah point of view.

TABLE 8.4
Rotated Factor Matrix: Varimax Rotation

Variable No. & Code	Factor 1 Being an Islamic Bank	Factor 2 Convenient Location	Factor 3 Loan Opportunity	Factor 4 Social Influence
1. PRSAV	0.75368			
2. NORIB	0.75253			
3. PLSINV	0.71271			
4. LNORIB	0.51088		0.51088	
5. ISLM	0.44997			
6. DHOME		0.71690		
7. PTRP		0.69410		
8. DWRK		0.65595		
9. PARK		0.62942		
10. BRCH		0.52159		
11. LOAN			0.88200	
12. TYPLON			0.87204	
13. ENFR				0.82401
14. PUBLIC				0.66631
Eigenvalue	3.88032	1.99714	1.42271	1.05374
% of Variance	27.7	14.3	10.2	7.5
Cumulative%	27.7	42.0	52.1	59.7

PRSAV (profits paid on savings); NORIB (no interest on savings); PLSINV (profit-sharing investments); LNORIB (no interest on loans); ISLM (runs on Islamic principles); DHOME (distance from home); PTRP (public transport convenience); DWRK (distance from work); PARK (parking facilities available); BRCH (number of branches available); LOAN (opportunity to get loan); TYPLON (types of loans offered); ENFR (encouragement of relatives & friends); PUBLIC (bank opening publicity).

Sources: Survey Finding.

Another important aspect of the depositors' behaviour that can be derived from Table 8.5 is the relatively high importance attached to the savings account. This is indicated by the median (3 = quite strong) for the "no interest on savings" (NORIB) and the "profits paid on savings" (PRSAV) variables. Of the depositors, 58 per cent and 55.7 per cent were at least quite strongly influenced by the two variables respectively. This implies that on the whole a majority of depositors were motivated by religious incentive to avoid *riba* and the monetary incentive to earn profits paid on their savings. The fact that savings account attracts the most number of depositors[10] may be partly explained by this finding.

TABLE 8.5
Degree of Influence: Factor 1 Variables

Degree of Influence	Value	ISLM (%)	PRSAV (%)	NORIB (%)	PLSINV (%)	LNORIB (%)
None	1	4.3	34.3	37.6	59.0	68.6
Little	2	1.4	7.6	6.7	6.2	8.5
Quite Strong	3	10.0	11.4	8.1	4.3	4.8
Strong	4	44.8	32.4	30.0	19.0	9.5
Very Strong	5	39.5	14.3	17.6	11.5	8.6
Cumulative (%)	–	94.3	58.1	55.7	34.8	22.9
Median Value	–	4	3	3	1	1
Mode Value	–	4	1	1	1	1

Since the variables are ordinal, the median is the most appropriate measure of central tendency.
Sources: Survey Finding.

In contrast to the savings account, the profit-sharing investment account did not seem to attract many depositors. Only 34.8 per cent were at least strongly influenced by it. Two plausible explanations may account for such behaviour. Firstly, the concept of profit-sharing accounts based on *mudarabah* is relatively new to many Malaysian Muslims. Unless one is familiar with Islamic economics or Islamic studies, the term is quite unknown to the ordinary man in the street. This is supported by our finding that 60 per cent of depositors have never heard of the investment account facility. To some extent, this reflects the poor marketing efforts of BIMB in promoting a new product which has the potential of giving the bank an advantage in the market. Secondly, the unpopularity of the investment account among individual Muslim depositors may also be attributed to the minimum investment deposit requirement of RM500, which is rather high for the medium income earner. Generally, Malaysian Muslims are low or medium income earners who can only afford to save small portions of their income. The more suitable investment outlets for such savings would be the National Unit Trust Scheme (Amanah Saham Nasional) or the Tabung Haji (Haji Fund). An Amanah Saham Nasional (ASN) investment can be made with as little as RM10. Tabung Haji, on the other hand, accepts small amounts of deposit through the various saving schemes and converts the pool of savings into investments.

It is because of the high minimum deposit requirement it was envisaged that those who were highly influenced by the investment account facility would be the high income earners. This is confirmed by the result of the Kruskall-Wallis non-parametric test (Table 8.6) which shows that the mean degree of influence of the high income group exceeds that of the low and medium income earners. Thus in contrast to the ASN scheme which aims to pool small Malay investments, it seems that the BIMB investment account has been tailored for those in the high income category. There is indeed a need for the management of BIMB to consider devising other forms of 'affordable' investment schemes for medium income earners. Such schemes would provide some means for these Muslims to channel their savings into profitable investments, particularly so since we found that 60 per cent of the respondents interviewed were still reluctant to invest in the ASN.

Regarding the influence of the LNORIB variable, only 22.9 per cent were motivated by the interest-free loans offered by BIMB. It is likely that many depositors were still ignorant of the new concepts of Islamic financing introduced by the bank. It is found that only those who received loans from the bank were highly influenced by this factor.

TABLE 8.6
Kruskall-Wallis Test:
Mean Ranks of PLSINV between Income Groups

PLSINV	Income Groups	Cases	Mean Rank	Significance
	RM1,401 & over	39 (21.7%)	k1 = 108.9	0.0096
	RM701–1,400	74 (41.1%)	k2 = 89.5	
	RM700 & below	67 (37.2%)	k3 = 80.8	

Table 8.4 earlier on also shows that the second important factor that has attracted depositors to BIMB is its convenient location. Variables such as the distance of the bank from their homes and workplaces, the number of branches and the availability of parking facilities have clustered under Factor 2. The lower eigenvalue and variance indicate that these variables were considered secondary by the BIMB depositors. It is found that only about 30–39 per cent of these depositors were at least quite strongly influenced by these variables. However, 45.7 per cent of depositors were quite strongly influenced by the availability of public transport, suggesting that the bank should at least be easily accessible.

It may be worth noting that studies on bank selection decisions conducted separately in the United States have shown that bank customers are mainly motivated by "convenience" in their bank selection decisions. Kaufman reported that convenience and the quality of services were considered most important by customers in selecting a primary bank.[11] Bowers also found that the convenient location of banks from both home and workplace were considered most important by households when selecting their primary banks.[12] The findings of both studies, however, do not seem to apply to the depositors of BIMB. Close to

61 per cent of depositors were not concerned by the distance of BIMB from their workplaces and this is attested by the fact that 73.4 per cent (94) of them worked in places located more than two miles from the bank. It can therefore be inferred that locational convenience did not really matter to most BIMB depositors. Many of them were willing to travel some distances to enjoy the satisfaction of avoiding *riba* in their banking transactions.

Other dominant factors have also emerged in more recent studies on bank selection decisions. For example, in the study by Anderson, Cox and Fulcher[13] the factor "recommendation by friends" was ranked more influential than "locational convenience". This finding is supported by another study by Tan which reported that consumers in Singapore tend to follow the advice of friends, neighbours and family giving less importance to convenience when selecting a bank.[14] Chua, on the other hand, found that Malaysian depositors in urban areas tend to attach high importance on the financial services (including rates of interest on deposits and loans) besides convenience and social influence.[15] These factors have also emerged in our findings. However, as indicated in Table 8.4, social influence ranked fourth in importance. It is found that only 32 per cent of these Muslim depositors have been at least strongly influenced by their relatives or friends to bank with BIMB. In terms of financial services, only 27.6 per cent of the depositors were at least strongly influenced by the opportunity to get loans from BIMB and 30.9 per cent by the types of loans offered. It is found that depositors who rated highly for Factor 3 were those who have managed to secure loans from BIMB and this constituted only 10 per cent of the sample.

In summary, Muslims in the urban areas are attracted to BIMB mainly because it offers an Islamic alternative which is fundamentally different from the traditional bank in terms of its operation and the types of services offered. The influence of contextual factors such as locational convenience and easy accessibility are of secondary in importance while social influence plays a less important role in determining depositors' preference for BIMB. These findings show that an Islamic bank operating side by side with a relatively developed conventional banking system can still create its own niche in the market for pious Muslims who are committed in avoiding *riba.* The bank selection decisions of these Muslims are fundamentally different from the typical conventional bank customer. The motivation to avoid *riba* surpasses all other factors in their bank selection decision. An important question that arises, however, is whether Islamic banking can go beyond this captive group of depositors and penetrate further into the market, especially in attracting other Muslims who currently bank only with interest-based banks.

Analysis of Muslim Depositors of *Riba* Banks

This group of Muslims forms a segment of the market which is still uncaptured by Islamic banking. It seems that the religious factor is not a sufficient motivation for them to bank with BIMB. A possible reason why these Muslims continue banking with conventional banks even after the establishment of BIMB could be their ignorance of the Islamic ban on *riba* and its modern connotations. It is possible that some of these Muslims may have never heard of the word *riba* before. On the other hand, those who knew that *riba* was forbidden may not know exactly what *riba* was. The absence of a clear-cut *fatwa* in relation to the controversy between *riba* and interest complicates the matter further.

Our findings, however show, that 99 per cent of this group were not ignorant of the word *riba.* However, only less than half of them (45.2 per cent) understood that interest was similar with *riba.* The rest of them were either unsure (32.7 per cent) or did not agree (22 per cent) that both interest and *riba* were prohibited in Islam. This implies that a high proportion of Muslim depositors of interest-based banks did not have a clear understanding of the true concept of *riba.* Their willingness to continue banking with the interest-based banks may be partly explained by this ignorance.

Given such ignorance, it is assumed that these Muslims were relatively less committed in avoiding *riba* in their banking transactions. At the outset we hypothesized that they were not attracted to BIMB because of the lower rates of return on deposits offered. However, on the contrary, it is found that only a very small percentage of depositors did not bank with BIMB's because of the lower rates of return on savings. It seemed that the rate of return was not the main reason these depositors did not bank with BIMB. Instead they were mainly discouraged by the lack of ATM service and the limited number of BIMB branches available. Less than 1 per cent of the depositors indicated to have been disappointed by the lower rates of return offered by BIMB compared with 43.9 per cent who were generally discouraged by the lack of ATMs and branches of BIMB. This finding suggests that this group of Muslims preferred conventional banks over BIMB for the same reasons that a majority of BIMB depositors maintained their accounts with conventional banks.

Bank Selection Criteria

The preceding result seems to imply that in the absence of the religious motivation, the bank selection decisions of Muslims who bank entirely with the conventional banks may not be different from that of the typical conventional bank depositors. To determine whether this is true, the bank selection determinants of the interest-based bank depositors were identified by factor analysis. Fifteen variables were analysed which produced four major factors (Table 8.7).

The emergence of "convenience" as the main bank selection determinant (Factor 1) for the Muslim depositors of interest-based banks seems to support the findings of Kaufman and Bowers which implies that the selection criteria of Muslim depositors conform to that of the typical conventional bank customer. The clustering of variables such as "many branches" (BRCH) and "distance from work" (DWRK) indicate the importance of locational convenience of the interest-based banks to these depositors. The "availability of automated teller machines" (ATM) and "fast counter service" (FASTSV) denotes, on the other hand, the importance of transactional convenience. The "well-known bank" variable may also be indirectly associated with convenience in the wider sense. The relatively strong weight of this variable in Factor 1 may be attributed to depositors' great concern for the safety of their deposits.

TABLE 8.7

Rotated Factor Matrix

Variable No. & Code	Factor 1 Convenience	Factor 2 Easily Accessible	Factor 3 Products Offered	Factor 4 Social Influence
1. BRCH	0.77907			
2. ATM	0.70021			
3. WLKNWN	0.61993			
4. DWRK	0.55849			
5. FASTSV	0.50219			
6. DEMPLY	–			
7. PTRP		0.78028		
8. DSHOP		0.71517		
9. PARK		0.71426		
10. TYPLON			0.87575	
11. LOAN			0.87138	
12. RSAV			0.54213	
13. ENCFR				0.88646
14. ADVERT				0.66274
15. DHOME				–
Eigenvalue	4.69568	1.80169	1.31622	1.02990
% of Variance	31.3	12.0	8.8	6.9
Cumulative%	31.3	43.3	52.1	59.0

ENCFR (encouragement of relatives/friends); BRCH (number of branches available); ATM (automated teller machines available); WLKNWN (well-known bank); DWRK (distance from work);

FASTSV (fast counter service); DEMPLY (salary paid in this bank); PTRP (public transport convenience); DSHOP (distance from where I shop); PARK (parking facilities available); TYPLON (types of loans offered); LOAN (opportunity to get loans); RSAV (rate of interest on savings); ADVERT (advertisements); DHOME (distance from home).
Sources: Survey Finding.

In the light of the scandals of the deposit-taking co-operatives and the collapse of a few commercial banks during the recession of 1980s it is plausible that depositors consider it important and convenient to deposit their money in banks which are well known and have a good business reputation. The label "convenience" is therefore justified to represent the variables in Factor 1 in the broad sense.

It is also evident that 84 per cent of these Muslims placed high importance on the extensive branch network, 82 per cent on the distance of the bank from their workplace, 80 per cent on the availability of electronic banking or ATMs, and 73.5 per cent on fast counter services. (Table 8.8). The high percentages denote that these depositors are purely convenience-oriented customers who demand fast and efficient banking services.

Our findings also show that even though a majority of the *riba* bank depositors were working in locations very near to BIMB, they still preferred the interest-based banks because of their ATM facility and the extensive branch networks.

We tested the null hypothesis to find out if any relationship existed among the DWRK, ATM and BRCH variables. The results of the cross-tabulation indicate that of the 140 depositors who were influenced by the convenient location of the bank from their workplaces, 79.3 per cent were also influenced by the ATM service and the extensive branch network factors. The null hypothesis of no association between the ATM, BRCH and DWRK variables can be rejected at the 0.05 level of statistical significance which implies that depositors are indeed simultaneously influenced by these three variables in deciding their preference for conventional interest-based banks.

TABLE 8.8

Degree of Influence: Factor 1 Variables

Degree of Influence	Value	BRCH (%)	DWRK (%)	ATM (%)	FASTSV (%)	WLKNWN (%)
None	1	9.4	11.2	14.7	15.9	18.8
Little	2	6.5	6.4	5.3	10.6	4.7
Cumulative (%)	–	15.9	17.6	20.0	26.5	23.5
Quite Strong	3	11.2	11.2	7.1	37.6	16.5
Strong	4	51.8	41.8	54.1	28.8	43.5
Very Strong	5	21.1	29.4	18.8	7.1	16.5
Cumulative (%)	–	84.1	82.4	80.0	73.5	76.5

Sources: Survey Finding.

In terms of locational convenience from workplaces (DWRK), the demographic profile of depositors who were strongly influenced by this factor were rather distinct. This group tends to be between 26 and 40 years old, working within two miles from the bank, with college or university education and are usually professionals or executives earning above average income. (Table 8.9). While it is rather self-evident that only depositors who are of working age and working near the banks will be necessarily more influenced by the DWRK variable, it is interesting to note that the more affluent depositors tend to be more influenced by this variable compared with the lower income or the lesser educated depositors. This tendency seems to suggest that depositors with higher socio-economic status are the most convenience-oriented Muslim depositors of interest-based banks. They regard banking as a convenience good and it is an important criteria for a bank to be conveniently located near their workplaces.

In terms of transactional convenience, an almost similar category of depositors were also highly influenced by the ATM facility of the secular interest-based banks. Depositors between the ages of 18 and 25 were the most influenced; followed by the majority who were 26–40 years old. Those over 40 were the least influenced. The influence of the ATM was also greatest among the convenience-oriented professionals and semi-professionals compared with depositors in the other professions.

TABLE 8.9

Kruskall-Wallis and U-Test: Mean Ranks of DWRK in Terms of Age, Distance from Work, Education, Income and Occupation

Variable	Subgroup	Cases	Mean Rank	Significance
	Age			
	18–25	41 (24.1%)	k1 = 71.21	
	26–40	111 (65.3%)	k2 = 96.13*	0.0002
	41 and above	18 (10.6%)	k3 = 52.50	
Distance	Far from Work (miles)			
from Work	0–2	135 (79.4%)	k4 = 93.6*	
	3–5	15 (8.8%)	k5 = 54.07	
	15 and further	20 (11.8%)	k6 = 54.33	0.0000
	Education		U-Test	
	Secondary	85 (50.0%)	u1 = 77.88	
	College/Univ.	85 (50.0%)	u2 = 93.12*	0.0331
	Income			
	RM700 & below	59 (36.6%)	k7 = 67.59	
	RM701–1,400	53 (32.9%)	k8 = 86.66	0.0199
	Over RM1,401	49 (30.5%)	k9 = 91.02*	
	Occupation			
	Prof/Exec	85 (53.1%)	k10= 87.7*	0.0209
	Clerical	47 (29.4%)	k11= 78.82	
	Unskilled etc.	28 (17.5\%)	k12= 61.38	

Sources: Survey Finding.

This finding agrees closely with the results of an earlier comparative study of ATM and non-ATM users in Malaysia which showed that active ATM users in Malaysia tend to be "highly educated, aged between 25 and 34 years with above average income."[16] It was also reported in the study that unlike the inactive cardholder, the active ATM users tend to "rely less on the traditional ways of conducting financial transaction" through the bank counters. Assuming that the Muslim depositors who were strongly influenced by the ATM service also behave in the same manner, it would explain further why they were not interested to bank with BIMB which lacked such a facility.

Factor 2 represents another aspect of convenience which is related to the easy accessibility of the bank either by public or private transport and its proximity to shopping centres. The most important variable, however, was public transport convenience as 60 per cent of these depositors reported to be quite strongly influenced by this variable. We were also able to distinguish depositors who were most influenced by this variable in terms of their level of education, income and occupation.

The results of the non-parametric tests show that depositors who were less educated, with lower income and employed in clerical or unskilled jobs were more influenced by the easy accessibility of interest-based banks compared with their respective counterparts. The importance of public transport convenience to these small savers may serve as a useful indication to the management of BIMB in determining the establishment of its mini-branches in the lower income states.

Factor 3 represents the influence of financial services offered by the interest-based banks and is comprised of three variables, namely, the type of loan offered, the opportunity to get loans and the rate of interest on savings. Since it is the third important factor extracted, its influence on the Muslim depositors' preference for interest-based banks is relatively less significant. More than half (51.2 per cent) of these Muslim depositors were not influenced at all by the types of loans offered by the interest-based banks. Similarly, 55.3 per cent were not concerned at all with the opportunity to secure loans from these banks and only 39.4 per cent regarded the rate of return paid on their savings account relatively important. A plausible reason for this attitude may be explained by the fact that more than half of these depositors (54.7 per cent) were public sector employees who were more likely to make use of the government housing loan facility rather than borrow from the interest-based banks. The current 1994 interest rate charged by the government on such loans is 4 per cent per year which is far lower than that charged by banks in general. This finding further supports the fact that individual Muslim depositors bank primarily with interest-based banks due to convenience rather than to earn interest.

This finding, however, differs from that of an earlier study by Chua[17] which examined the bank selection decisions of Malaysian households of an urban residential area near Kuala Lumpur. The study, which was carried out on a sample consisting of 68 per cent non-Malays, revealed that "financial services offered" by conventional banks—which included loans, overdrafts and the rate of interest on deposits—were rated most important relative to convenience and social influence. The difference between our results and that of Chua indirectly shows that different marketing strategies may have to be applied by BIMB to attract different groups of potential depositors to Islamic banking. While the promotional appeals emphasizing on relative rates of return on deposits may be the most effective approach to attract non-Muslims to Islamic banks, the provision of convenience banking may be quite sufficient to induce the less strict Muslims to shift their funds from the conventional commercial banks to an Islamic bank.

Corresponding to our earlier findings on the bank selection criteria of BIMB depositors, it is also found that social influence plays a less important role in the bank selection decision of Muslim depositors of the interest-based banks. Social influence is ranked fourth in importance.

While less than 30 per cent of depositors were socially influenced in selecting their present bank, about 28.9 per cent have been at least moderately motivated by the banks' advertising promotions and a lesser proportion (21.2 per cent) have been encouraged by their relatives or friends. Therefore, from the analysis of the four factors above we can conclude that:

1. The factors influencing the bank selection decisions of Muslims who bank primarily with the interest-based banks are quite similar with those of the conventional bank depositors although the importance attributed to some of those factors may differ between the two groups. The Muslim individuals were highly influenced by both locational and transactional convenience and to a lesser extent by the accessibility of public transport, the products and financial services offered and social influence.
2. The main attraction of the interest-based banks to their Muslim depositors is the combination of an extensive branch network, their convenient location from the depositors' workplaces and the availability of ATM service.
3. Depositors with high education, high income and professional positions tend to be highly convenience-oriented and are strongly influenced by the convenient location of the interest-based banks from their workplace and the transactional convenience provided by the ATMs.
4. The impact of the ATM facility is greatest among the younger depositors, which implies that its importance will remain high as the current population ages.
5. The rates of return on deposits and the types of loans are relatively unimportant to most Muslim depositors of conventional banks.
6. On the whole, convenience is the prime reason Muslim depositors bank primarily with conventional banks.

Conclusion

Perhaps one of the most important market implications that emerges from the preceding analysis is the limited ability of BIMB to provide convenience banking to attract patronage from a wider section of the Muslim population. While the religious motivation factor may be sufficient to sustain patronage from the existing depositors of BIMB, we have identified that both locational convenience in the form of extensive branch networks and transactional convenience through ATMs are important to Muslims who currently bank exclusively with the conventional banks.

The present package of Islamic banking services offered by BIMB does not seem to fulfil the banking needs of these Muslims. Hence, even though existing BIMB branches may be conveniently located in the same area as the interest-based banks the lack of the ATM service and the limited number of branches puts BIMB at a disadvantage in the competition for deposits from these convenience-oriented Muslims. Our findings also show that these convenience-oriented Muslims are of high net worth, belonging to the high income group. These are potential depositors who should be the main targets of BIMB in devising its marketing strategies.

As a new player in the market, BIMB is indeed very far behind in the competition for deposits through its branches. Its current branch network cannot match the convenience of branch banking that the four well-known top banks in Malaysia are providing to their depositors. The top two commercial banks have over a hundred branches all over the country some reaching remote rural areas. Bank Islam Malaysia, in contrast, can only take pride of its network of over thirty branches. It seems that BIMB does not have much to offer in terms of branch banking.

In terms of ATM banking, BIMB is one of the few banks which does not offer such services to its depositors. Even though its management had announced its intention to install ATMs in mid-1992,[18] the project is still in its pilot stage. Yet, even the medium-sized banks in BIMB's peer group have started offering this service using the shared ATM networks. This indicates that all banks in the urban areas consider the provision of the ATM service essential to attract depositors—BIMB is no exception. The introduction of ATM service is important not only to attract new depositors but also to maintain the loyalty of existing depositors who still hold supplementary accounts in the interest-based banks. It is envisaged that with the introduction of the ATMs these depositors would close these accounts and bank exclusively with BIMB.

Another important market implication is the impact of the establishment of Islamic counters by the conventional banks. Our survey findings show that both the depositors of BIMB and of *riba* banks welcome such moves. While BIMB depositors anticipated the religious benefit in terms of the avoidance of *riba* as the prime benefit followed by convenience and competition which would improve the quality of consumer services, the conventional bank depositors foresee the opportunity to evade interest without having to give up the convenience that they currently enjoy from the conventional banks. Here again we see that convenience is considered relatively important by the conventional bank depositors compared with the depositors of BIMB. As more conventional banks begin to open Islamic counters, the eventuality of fierce competition for customers is inevitable; with BIMB being the likely end loser. This outcome is most probable for a few reasons. Firstly, the fulfilment of the current unmet demand for Islamic banking services in rural areas are likely to be led by the Islamic counters rather than BIMB. This is because of the more extensive branch networks of the interest-based banks, giving these banks a comparative advantage to capture the rural market and involving less operating cost than BIMB. Secondly, unless BIMB comes out of its cocoon and embark on more aggressive marketing strategies to match the convenience facilities offered by the *riba* banks in the urban areas, the chances of BIMB in attracting new deposits from the *riba* banks seems remote. In addition, there is also a real threat that the bank may not be able to stop the outflow of its existing deposits into the Islamic counters of these banks. These will bear serious implications on the market share of BIMB, both in the urban and rural areas.

Nevertheless, BIMB can still create a niche in the market by improving on its corporate image. To many people, the current image of BIMB as an Islamic bank is below expectations, especially in its utilization of funds. The bank's concentration on "mark-up financing" and the relatively high mark-up charged, have left many Malaysian Muslims disillusioned. It seems the major obstacle lies in the prolonged reluctance of the bank's management to undertake risk in the form of profit-sharing ventures even though the Malaysian economy has already come out of the recession and is heading for high economic growths in the 1990s. After being in the market for ten years and coupled by the increase in the bank's capital base as well as its public listing in the Kuala Lumpur Stock Exchange, the "infant bank" argument is no longer valid to justify BIMB's current financing policy. The favourable economic environment and the current industrialization policy provide a golden opportunity for BIMB to test the ground with *musharakah* long-term financing. The bank can create a niche in financing small- and medium-sized industries (SMIs) with good projects but which lacked collateral to secure loans from conventional banks. The concern for viability and profitability is one of the main selling points of Islamic banking[19] and in the context of the SMIs this would appeal to the more enterprising and innovative entrepreneurs. The prospects of securing long-term equity financing which is less burdensome and more just would induce them to bank with the Islamic bank. In other words, another route for BIMB to attract new deposits and hence increase its market share is by offering Islamic financing facilities which are more superior than the *riba*-based loans of the conventional banks in terms of economic justice, resource allocation and distribution.

An important prerequisite, however, is the need for the immediate establishment of a marketing research and development department by the bank. This is because equity financing requires the bank to be highly selective in the identification of its partners and projects to be financed. In relation to this, the recruitment of trained personnel to appraise potential projects and monitor the progress of approved projects must also be immediately addressed by the bank.

Finally an important policy implication that emerges from this study is the need to educate the public about the principles of Islamic banking and finance and the different types of services that can be offered by the Islamic bank. Since the present government aims to develop a dual banking system whereby the new Islamic banking system will complement the existing conventional banking structure it is only relevant that the awareness of the new system and a knowledge of Islamic financing methods should be promoted via the education system at the national level, and the corporate level through lectures, seminars and workshops. This approach would be a more effective way of explaining the complexity of *mudarabah* and *musharakah* compared with advertisements which would only generate short-lived interest in the Islamic banking products that is being marketed. At present, Muslims are generally ignorant of the banking services that are available at BIMB. To a society which has only known debt-financing as the only method of borrowing from banks it is essential to educate them on the new concepts of profit sharing, partnerships, deferred payment sale, leasing and mark-up sale. The lack of understanding of the bank's concepts and operations have also led many to think that an Islamic bank is a welfare organization not a financial institution.

In conclusion, the challenge for BIMB to create a niche in the Malaysian market depends on how far it can fulfil the needs of its customers. The first issue that needs to be addressed is how it can match the conventional banks in terms of the quality of banking services offered. Secondly, BIMB would have to devise financing instruments which are more just to cater not only for the rich industrialists but also for the majority of small Muslim entrepreneurs in the urban areas, the farmers and the fishermen in rural areas as well as the other middle and low income earners. The most effective way of identifying the needs of these different market segments is through market research from which the most appropriate marketing strategies can be formulated.

Notes

1 R. Abdul Kader, *Performance and Market Implications of Islamic Banking: A Case Study of Bank Islam Malaysia Bhd.*, unpublished Ph.D. thesis, University of Durham, United Kingdom, 1993.

2 Malayan Banking Bhd., Bank Bumiputra Malaysia Bhd., United Malaysian Bank Corporation and Public Bank Bhd.

3 The 'random arrival' method of sampling was adopted by which the daily banking opening hours were divided into one hour intervals. A respondent was randomly selected to answer a questionnaire at half-hour intervals.

4 Z. Man, "Islamic Banking: The Malaysian Experience," in M. Ariff (ed.), *Islamic Banking in South East Asia Institute of South East Asian Studies*, Singapore, 1988.

5 Of the RM77,589 million total domestic commercial bank deposits mobilized as at December 31, 1992, the market share of Bank Islam Malaysia was RM1,331 million or 1.7 per cent of the total: Bank Negara Annual Report 1992.

6 U.A, Aziz, *Pilgrims Economy Improvement Plan*, Kuala Lumpur, 1959.

7 Ibid., p.87.

8 M.J. Norusis, *SPSSX: Advance Statistics Guide*, McGraw Hill, New York, 1985.

9 This is a rotated factor matrix which is crucial to interpret the results of the factor analysis. The interpretation of the four factors being extracted would be based on the loadings of the 14 variables on these factors. Each factor loading is the correlation coefficient which shows how much weight is assigned to that factor. Hence, the factor loading of 0.71690 in the sixth row of the second column indicates the strength of the correlation between the variable DHOME (distance from home) and Factor 2. The label for each factor can be defined in accordance to the variables which load most highly with it. Hence, Factor 2 can be labeled as "Convenient Location". It is also worth noting that variables with factor loadings 0.3 are considered insignificant and are usually ignored.

10 There were about 230,000 savings account depositors in 1990, representing 85 per cent of the bank's total depositors.

11 G. Kaufman, "Customers View Bank Markets and Services: A survey of Elkhart, Indiana," a report to the Federal Reserve Bank, Chicago, 1969.

12 R. Bowers, "Businesses, Households and Their Banks," *Business Review*, March 1969.

13 W. Anderson, P. Cox and D. Fulcher, "Bank Selection Decisions and Market Segmentation," *Journal of Marketing*, 40, January 1976.

14 Tan Chin Tong, "A Case Study of Bank Selection Decisions and Market Segmentation," an unpublished report, University of Singapore.

15 Chua A.L., *Factors Influencing Bank Selection Decision by Consumers in Petaling Jaya*, an MBA dissertation, University of Malaya, 1989.

16 Reported by Oliver Ho, "Consumer Behaviour for the Banking Industry," *Bankers Journal*, Malaysia, December 1987.

17 Ibid.

18 *Berita Harian*, June 30, 1991.

19 Muhammad K. Ariff, "Islamic Banking in Malaysia: Framework, Performance and Lessons," *Journal of Islamic Economics*, 2 (2), July 1989.

Chapter 9

Islamic Consultancy House

SAAD AL-HARRAN

THROUGHOUT THE LAST decade, Malaysia enjoyed rapid foreign investments by various sources. The main reason many foreign manufacturers have established factories to manufacture various products was mainly due to the relatively low labour cost, conducive investment environment, political stability, preferential treatment for foreign capital, an educated labour force, positive stance of improving infrastructure and consistent economic policy.

Undoubtedly, the Malaysian government's consistent economic policy is the key factor behind the foreign investors' investment decision. This policy has played an important role in accelerating both industrialization and growth into export bases of manufactured goods. Another factor is the growth of domestic consumption accompanying the rise in per capita national income. This virtuous cycle in which investment and individual consumption expand together, has created the market for the investors more than the consumers.

During the 1990s there has been a slowdown in the inflow of foreign investments to Malaysia as shown by the fall to just RM1.4 billion in the first five months of 1993 from RM4.4 billion in the previous year's corresponding period. This downtrend is due to external factors: mainly the recession in the West and Japan. Being the main investor in

Malaysia, Japan, for instance, after the new government came to power made some economic decisions which affected Malaysia. One such decision was that, to improve the economic and financial climate in their country, domestic investment was to be given top priority rather than external investment.

The question to be asked is how can Malaysia break the vicious circle of foreign investment and the mobilization of domestic resources. Should she continue depending on foreign investments? Or should it mobilize her domestic resources internally before it is too late?

This chapter intends to raise the following questions:

1. Why is there an urgent need now to utilize domestic resources for investment purposes?
2. Is Malaysia really in urgent need of foreign investment? Or is it the problem of surplus funds (more than the shortage of capital) which the corporate sector is currently facing?
3. What will be the role of an Islamic consultancy house (ICH) in utilizing the surplus funds in the corporate sector for financing viable projects to achieve economic and financial independence and realizing the leadership vision of year 2020?

Utilization of Domestic Resources

No doubt the mobilization of domestic resources requires policies to facilitate the process of capital accumulation. The final goal of development programme is to find the best way of breaking the vicious circle of capital shortage and underdevelopment, and to design the most efficient and optimum rate of capital accumulation.

It would be an oversimplification to regard economic development as a matter of capital accumulation alone. The other factors required are, for example, entrepreneurship and training of workers and public administrators. Yet these are seldom possible without some increase in the stock of capital.[1] Capital increases through investment, and more investments necessitate more savings. Domestic savings are, therefore, the more reliable source of investment to break the vicious circle of poverty and underdevelopment. But domestic savings can only be increased by cutting down on consumption which has to be compared with the future increases in consumption it promises. Investment yields different returns depending on the industries in which it is made.

Problem of Surplus Funds

This is a problem that most banks, including merchant and Islamic banks, are facing. This might be due to the lack of long-term vision and the banker's perception that long-term financing are risky investments and should therefore be avoided. The investment strategy of these institutions were set up to give due consideration only to short-term financing through *murabaha* and *mudarabah*. Long-term financing (which Islamic banks have to undertake through *musharakah* financing) will re-quire commitment, dedication and hard work to make the projects successful and profitable. Unlike traditional banks, the anxieties of an Islamic bank start after it gives out funds for investment: it would have to follow up on the project to which finance was provided to see that it has been spent in the proper way and that the project is well managed. This introduces the need for a very strong follow-up department. Its participating members should be active partners in the business; they should have mutual interest to make the project successful and well qualified to serve and deal with and advise different types of people and businesses. The following up does not only ensure efficient utilization of finance and guarantees a sizeable return on the investment, but also looks after the efficient performance of the concerned business.[2]

Now since the initial viability has been established, Islamic banking has really come of age. It needs to come out of the safe pastures of "soft investment" and of socially desirable long-term projects. For an Islamic bank to finance long-term projects certain prerequisites must be met: they will have to identify these projects, carry out technical feasibility studies, estimate expected streams of profits and only then will they invest in those projects.[3] Moreover, they would have to develop a long-term investment strategy and would be expected to show more social responsibility in this regard by ensuring socially productive use of their resources.

The Role of an Islamic Consultancy House

No doubt, the promotion of small and medium scale enterprises is essential for promoting entrepreneurial talents in Malaysia. The problem that policymakers are facing is to determine how best to promote entrepreneurial talents and thus generate sufficient number of viable projects, particularly in small industries.

In meeting these challenges, an Islamic consultancy house (ICH) would consider the following initial two tasks of central importance. One, the establishment of close contact with the Ministry of International Trade and Industries and different States authorities through the opening of branch offices. And two, the identification of project ideas in the light of such natural and other resources, demand conditions and infrastructural facilities that would emerge over time.

The Strategy of the Islamic Consultancy House

The main objectives of the proposed ICH are based on the spirit of cooperation and trust which are related to individual and group behaviour in utilizing available funds in addition to other resources, in such a manner, to achieve a society of justice and fairness.

The strategy of the ICH relates to

a. Identification of the interrelated functions that require to be performed in a certain sequential order for an effective and efficient promotional role;
b. A mechanism for making effective decisions; and
c. The institutional machinery required to perform the various functions identified.

An ICH identifies the interrelated functions essential for its promotional role as follows:

a. Identification and selection of the project;

b. Preparation of the preliminary feasibility study;
c. Identification of entrepreneurs to undertake these projects;
d. Provision of training to potential entrepreneurs;
e. Preparation of detailed project reports;
f. Provision of technical and financial assistance for projects ready for implementation;
g. Monitoring and following up of projects;
h. Managerial and technical assistance for operating enterprises with problems; and
i. Technical appraisal of projects requiring further financial assistance.

The Philosophy of the Islamic Consultancy House

The philosophy of ICH is based on the concept of partnership in business because it aims at achieving the ultimate goal and objective of Islamic finance. Any taskforce mission should simultaneously meet these basic conditions and qualifications:

a. Responsibility;
b. Accountability;
c. Hard work; and
d. Time value.

As shown above, having a strong and firm belief which takes into account the qualities of responsibility, accountability, hard work and time value is vital to make a project a success or failure. The other important aspects in project financing which the active partners have to take into consideration are trustworthiness, co-operation, frankness, communication and delegation of power (decentralization). Lastly, incentives are the motivating factor that cannot be ignored and may lead to the project success. Among the types of incentives are financial interdependence and a higher standard of living.

The first step to be taken is a reconnaissance mission regarding the proposed project to identify its viability. The following step is applied research and this will require a preparation of the questionnaire-based survey of the potential business area. This requires a taskforce which strongly holds the basic foundation of partnership financing system as mentioned above, namely, having belief, commitment coupled with the fact that they are offered with incentives. Once the questionnaire is analysed, a detailed feasibility study should be undertaken. It also requires a constant following up and monitoring by the partners to ensure its success.

Rationale for the Islamic Consultancy House Strategy

The basic question that arises in this connection is why the ICH has not been sponsored by the financial institutions? Clearly, there is an urgent need for ICH services: there are hardly any private consultancy services oriented and committed (to this mission) towards the proper development of small- and medium-scale industries in the country. Such services could emerge only when a market of adequate size is developed; but the market would not be adequate unless such services were provided.

The corporate sector has an urgent need for ICH services to appraise the technical aspects of projects submitted to them by entrepreneurs. Instead of each trying to build such technical expertise, it would obviously be economical to have access to it in an ICH serving all the financial institutions. Furthermore, once the financial institutions begin stressing the technical aspects (appropriate adaptation of products, processes and equipment to the local environment) they would introduce a demand for ICH services by the existing and the new enterprises that seek financial assistance from them. Finally, the promotional role would be more effective and efficient if the financial institutions themselves sponsor the ICHs. They would insist on firstly, an economic and financial viability not only of the ICH, but also of the promoted enterprises, and secondly, the orderly and balanced performance of functions so that one is related to the other in a balanced and sequential manner. For example, it is no use stressing project identification or feasibility studies if they do not result in feasible projects.

Conclusion and Recommendations

The problem of initiating a viable and profitable project particularly in developing countries, is a common phenomenon in all these economies. Development of small enterprises is essential for two main reasons: firstly, to develop latent entrepreneurial and managerial ability on a wide geographical and functional basis; and secondly, to create employment opportunities on a viable basis for whole communities, especially for lower skilled or lesser educated workers in the rural areas to improve the distribution of wealth and income.

It is generally recognized that merely fiscal and financial incentives are insufficient to set such a process in motion. What is required in addition is some institutional machinery, that is, Islamic consultancy houses for identifying financially viable projects and entrepreneurs, preparing feasibility studies, making appropriate technological choices, formulating detailed projects with specifications for plant and machinery, processes and products and providing assistance in project implementation, monitoring and following up.

The proposed Islamic Consultancy House sponsored by and linked with financial institutions is likely to attain its objectives more economically and effectively than one set up by the government. There are for several reasons for this. Firstly, the financial institutions need the services of the house in performing their promotional role and in the technical appraisal of projects for which financial assistance is sound. And secondly, they can induce entrepreneurs to use the services of the houses by insisting on the technical soundness of projects that require financial assistance.

In the final analysis, the major challenge that faces Malaysia has not been that due to the shortage of funds, but rather that due to surplus funds. The main difficulty is identifying sound and financially viable projects. The proposed ICH has certain functions and practical visions to achieve. It will undoubtedly play an active role in utilizing the surplus funds in the corporate sector, moving gradually and progressively towards long-term financing in order to curb capital flight from this country.

Notes

1 G.M. Meier, *Leading Issues in Economics Development*, Third Edition, Oxford University Press, New York, 1976, pp.252–258.

2 S. Al-Harran, *Islamic Banking: Managing the Challenges*, Institute for Policy Research, Monograph Series, 1992, pp.6–10.

3 S. Al-Harran, *Islamic Finance: Partnership Financing*, Pelanduk Publications, Petaling Jaya, 1993, pp.320–330.

Chapter 10

Marketing Research and the Corporate Sector

SAAD AL-HARRAN

WE ARE LIVING in the age of information technology and the world of computers is moving forward very fast indeed. The automated teller machine (ATM) was brought to us from the West to facilitate our daily financial transactions. One of the latest technology in the market today is the tele-banking services in which bank customers can literally do their banking at home through the telephone system. This would undoubtedly make the life of a household easier.

However, some questions should be asked: Why is the emphasis only on the technology, and what is the missing part? Will technology alone solve human problems or will it make our life even more complicated? In the contemporary corporate sector in Malaysia, we have seen and observed that the focal point is toward the technology (computers) rather than the human being. This is why some financial institutions have failed to achieve their social objectives and their main concern is to open up more branches in the country, thus increasing the transaction cost, which the consumers would have to pay. These institutions become inefficient in their work producing more paperwork rather then sound project proposal. Apparently the consumers are getting frustrated because their needs have not been fulfilled due to the unhealthy business environment prevailing in these institutions. Because of the consumers' awareness they made sound decisions to shift their funds to other institutions with the hope that they can get better service and care.

We are living in the age of human resource development and the current thinking in the Western corporate sector is how to develop close relationships between the financial institutions and their consumers. Their policymakers have advocated the concept of relationship investment. This means that the human being is a very important factor in the corporate policy planning. Their needs should be fulfilled if financial institutions want to stay competitive in the market.

In Islam (as way of life) the focal point is the man rather than the capital. Through proper education and practical training man can generate the capital for economic development. His needs as a consumer have to be understood and fulfilled by the financial institutions—thus the importance of marketing research to the corporate sector. Understanding the needs of the consumers requires serious efforts on the part of the corporate policymakers to be active and market oriented. Any business organization that wants to be competitive in the market must undertake applied marketing research. If their staff are not trained or equipped to do the job, they can assign this important responsibility to a marketing consultant. Every business that wants to survive in this age of competition must allocate large sums out of their funds for research and development (R&D). The policymakers may give this important assignment to university students through their active professors to be hired as consultants. Such an assignment will also give the students the chance to feel that they are a part of society rather than alien to it. The following practical steps should be taken:

1. The policymakers have to liaise with the relevant professor in the local universities to undertake this important assignment.
2. The professor of finance and banking, or marketing and business strategy should lead the mission. He has to be fully independent and a fund should be allocated for this kind of applied marketing research. He has to make his own selections based on certain criteria to develop a leadership among the students.

3. A reconnaissance marketing mission should be undertaken and the students should have as many ideas as possible from the market based on their interview of the public about the consumers' real needs.
4. Once the above task is accomplished, a questionnaire should be developed to help reflect the main needs of the consumers. Ultimately the data should be analysed through Statistical Packages for Social Science (SPSS).
5. Once the detailed report has been completed it will be forwarded to the concerned financial institution for evaluation and assessment.

Such an applied marketing research will be invaluable to corporate policymakers and students alike. For the students, it is a real-life practical experience. A financial reward should be given to them for their hard work and for understanding the concept of time management. They will be considered valuable human assets to the institution and perhaps the future employees once they complete their studies.

For financial institutions to be successful, the concept of sharing and caring should be introduced in their culture and day-to-day work. It is time for corporate policymakers to make changes in their perception and to consider investing in R&D. Therefore, marketing research should not only be conducted in the large cities but go beyond that, to the rural people who are also part of the society. This is where the real impact of the institution will be. It is not fair and just that credit should not be supplied to the rural people.

Credit is important to everyone, especially to the rural folk, for without credit they cannot survive. Without financing the farmers cannot cultivate land and feed their families. If credit cannot be provided by the formal financial institution (as in the case currently), then the farmers and the fishermen would have no alternative but to deal with the informal sector, which is powerful and controlled by the middlemen and the moneylenders. Due to this unhealthy environment prevailing in the rural areas we can understand why many farmers made the difficult decision to migrate to the large cities. And yet we should ask ourselves why are the prices of agricultural commodities continually increasing. Obviously, the main cause is the higher interest rate charged by the moneylenders to these people. In some countries like those in Africa the rate of interest can go as high as 60–70 per cent.

Truly, it is time for policymakers to restructure the rural economy based on fair play and justice by introducing the concept of Islamic finance, partnership financing, which is based on profit or loss sharing. This system has proven its success in other countries and can create harmony in the society. Finally, if the corporate sector wants to be a part of society, its moral responsibility would be to create a harmony in it by providing credit to everyone before it is too late.

Chapter 11

The Islamic Stock Exchange[1]

SAAD AL-HARRAN

IN THE CONTEMPORARY corporate world, the stock exchange plays an important role as financial intermediary between those who have surplus funds, and those who need the money. The former are the investors while the latter are the entrepreneurs. Therefore, the stock exchange is playing the role of a middleman or intermediary between these two parties. The Kuala Lumpur Stock Exchange (KLSE) is an organized market, and the two parties have to pay transaction costs for the services provided.

This chapter intends to

1. Analyse the current practices at the KLSE as a financial intermediary and identify the main beneficiaries;
2. Investigate whether Islam can bring an alternative to the current practices to create a healthy and conducive environment to the stock exchange; and
3. Propose the establishing of a small Islamic stock exchange (SISE) to cater for the needs of small- and medium-sized enterprises to enable them to raise funds for business expansion.

The KLSE is divided into two boards, namely, the Main Board and the Second Board. For the former, the requirement for a company to be listed is a minimum capital of RM20 million while for the later it is between RM5–20 million.

We must question whether this division of two main boards serve the needs of small- and medium-sized enterprises (SMEs) with less than RM5 million, whose main objectives are to raise funds (through KLSE) to expand their businesses. As far as we can see, the mechanism prevailing at the stock exchange does not only help the rich get richer but also make corporations bigger, more powerful, and monopolizing the wealth of the nation. Such practices, if not rectified by the relevant government authorities will sooner or latter make the stock exchange more alien to the society rather than part of it. This fact enhances the argument that we are indeed living in a world of unfairness and injustice: the world of the giant corporations where the "bigger fishes swallow the smaller ones."

In the KLSE, there are also two main players, namely, the genuine investors and the inside traders. For the former, the main reason for their involvement in the stock exchange is simply either to raise funds for business expansion or to make quick profits. Therefore, the investors have to work harder and study the macro-economic fundamentals as their starting point. They have to analyse the various factors that will affect their investment decisions at the second stage. These factors are unemployment rate, inflation, business cycle, rate of growth, interest rates, etc. Once a thorough assessment has been made (by themselves or by their investment consultants) on the macro-economic fundamental, the second stage starts: analysing the micro fundamentals of the chosen companies among which are, their growth rates and past records, dividends, sales turnover, profitability and other financial ratios.

For the latter (the inside traders), they are known to spread rumours in the stock exchanges. This kind of people usually do not work hard compared with their counterparts (the genuine investors). Their main objective is to make a fortune over a short period at the expense of others. They would release false information and cause panic to the whole stock exchange, and more specifically, to the genuine investors, to make them quickly sell off their shares. Moreover, we suspect that these rumours are usually started by some of the big corporations in the stock exchange to manipulate the market and force the genuine investors to go out of the stock market forever. Many investors think that the inside traders are a group of people who will be able to buy the shares at a bargain price at the expense of the investors. This is why large number of investors refuse to raise funds from the stock exchange (perhaps also for moral and ethical reasons) for business expansion while others feel that current stock exchanges are becoming more like casinos or gambling dens, and according to their beliefs and ethics, such practices are unlawful and should be avoided. Ironically, such a practise does not only prevail at KLSE but also in other stock exchanges (like the New York Stock Exchange) all over the world. It is indeed based on speculations and manipulations (internal and external factors) rather than economic and financial fundamentals.

The question should be asked: should we continue to have such unfair practices in the stock exchange where few are monopolizing the wealth of the nation at the expense of the others? Or is it the right time for the policymakers in the corporate sector to restructure the stock exchange by bringing changes and introducing new rules and regulations to safeguard the small investors and entrepreneurs. If such changes were introduced and enforced (by the relevant authorities) they will undoubtedly create a healthy environment for the whole financial market to exist. For the small investors, it will bring new hope and they will again be keen to be active players in the stock exchange either in buying or selling shares or by raising funds for business expansion.

An Islamic Alternative

Islam as a way of life can bring an alternative and create a healthy environment to the stock exchange. The most fundamental teaching that Islam advocates in any financial transactions is "you should not do harm to others while others should not do harm to you."

At the macro level, this dynamic concept has its own grass-root Islamic foundation. It is based on ethical and moral values rather than materialism. It is focused on the role of man in the society as vicegerents (*khilafah*) of God (the main Creator and the real owner of wealth and natural resources of the universe) on earth. God has given man the responsibility to test him; the life we are in is indeed a test by God to mankind. Everything in life is planned and well monitored by the Creator, and man will be accountable for his deeds and actions he has made in this life. According to Chapra, God-given resources are indeed a trust[2] and it should achieve the following objectives:

a. The resources are for the benefit of all, not just a few. They must be utilized equitably for the well-being of all.
b. Everyone must acquire resources rightfully and in accordance to the Quran and the Sunnah.
c. No one is authorized to destroy or waste the resources that God has given. To do so is equated by the Quran to the spreading of *fasad* (mischief and corruption) which God abhors.[3]

If man fully understands the real massage of Islam in life, he will live peacefully and in harmony with others based on the universal brotherhood.

Prophet Mohammad (May the peace and blessing of God be on him) said: "All human beings are dependents of God and the most beloved of them before Him are those who are best to His dependents."

He should be honest in dealing with others (realizing that God is monitoring him and there will be accountability afterwards) especially in any financial transaction. His main mission in life is hard work, responsibility, time management and sharing and caring for others. This is why Islam has given importance to the concept of universal brotherhood which implies unity, co-operation and partnership among mankind. It is indeed based on trust, honesty and mutual co-operation and co-ordination rather than hatred, selfishness and greed which is prevailing in the conventional corporate world.

Islam encourages people to compete with each other in every aspect of life—in business and commerce, education and research and development—to help develop a solid and healthy society. Competition raises efficiency and helps promote human well-being, the overall objective of Islam. A society of trust, moral and ethical values. Undoubtedly, for investors, an improvement in the quality of production means that they will have a market for their product not only for the local but also foreign market to sell their products. Ultimately, the consumers (who are the main target) will benefit, so does the society as a whole. Therefore, competition will create a healthy environment and encourage the investors and entrepreneurs to work harder to have a market for their products.

This is why Islam is in favour of competition and against monopoly. The latter can bring harm to mankind and to the society as a whole. The resources will be wasted and be used unproductively and ultimately it will be monopolized and controlled by a few hands at the expense of others. Monopoly usually means selfishness, greediness, and oversized institutions. This is why Islam advocates the concept of "small is beautiful." If the small business is well managed, closely monitored and followed up, it can bring benefit to the society. Once these entrepreneurs are motivated through partnership financing they will work harder and improve their standard of living. They have a mission in life, the first and foremost, being to seek the pleasure of the Creator (who has given them the opportunities and the responsibilities) and to bring happiness not only to their families but also to other people and prosperity to the whole society. These investors (or entrepreneurs) are keen to be bigger and their main objectives are maximization of social benefit rather than maximization of the profit.

In Islam, savers and investors are considered as one body. Once a viable project is submitted to them (for financing) by an Islamic investment company (IIC), who will identify and select the projects based on economic and financial merits, the savers will automatically become the investors of those projects. This dynamic formula explains why Islam encourages us to go for partnership financing and venture capital. It is a challenge, and life without it is indeed meaningless. Muslims should face the challenge to survive in the new economic order set in a world of injustice, exploitations, and hatred between those that have and those that have not. Therefore, Islam has advocated planning for long-term financing for the development of human beings rather than short-term gains to please only some of the rich.

Such a long-term mission will require the need to establish an Islamic consultancy house (ICH) to cater for the needs of the development of human resources. The strategy of the ICH relates to firstly, identification of the interrelated functions that should be performed in a certain sequential order for an effective and efficient promotional role; secondly, a mechanism for making effective decisions; and thirdly, the institutional machinery required to perform the various functions identified.

The ICH identifies the interrelated functions essential for its promotional role as follows:

a. Identification and selection of the project;
b. Preparation of the preliminary feasibility study;
c. Identification of entrepreneurs to undertake these projects;
d. Provision of training to potential entrepreneurs;
e. Preparation of detailed project reports;
f. Provision of technical and financial assistance for projects ready for implementation;
g. Monitoring and following up of projects;
h. Managerial and technical assistance for operating enterprises with problems; and
i. Technical appraisal of projects requiring further financial assistance.

Once a viable and feasible project has been identified by a competent Islamic practitioner (or the ICH), based on economic and financial merits, it can be sold directly to the savers (who will be automatically investors) without any intermediary. A profitable project with a high rate of return will automatically find its market in the corporate sector (through the computer networks and information technology) without any financial intermediary.

From the above analysis, one can say that in Islamic economics, the financial intermediation will have a limited role to play in the society. Through financial intermediary, transaction costs will ultimately be paid by the society and the cost of capital will be expensive for many small entrepreneurs who want to start their venture capital. The current economic and financial crisis in the Western world have undoubtedly demonstrated that in the age of recession many small entrepreneurs cannot survive and they have to close down their workshops and factories. Such persistent economic and financial problems will have an adverse affect on the society as a whole. The main causes for such a situation are transaction costs and interest rates. These people in the corporate world cannot grow simply because they cannot provide the collateral to the financial intermediaries (like the banks and other financial institutions).

Proposed Establishment of a Small Islamic Stock Exchange

From the above analyses, we are of the opinion that the policymakers in the government as well as corporate sector should study the proposal of establishing a small Islamic stock exchange (SISE) to cater for the needs of those small companies with smaller amounts of market capitalization requirement. Such a proposal is in line with the leadership Vision 2020 to promote the SMEs and make them more competitive and efficient. This proposal of establishing a SISE goes in line with Islamic principle where monopoly is prohibited and competition from all parties are encouraged. It is also important for the relevant authorities to set up a Securities Exchange Commission (SEC) to regulate the market so that a healthy environment will be created so that the "bigger fishes will not swallow the smaller ones." Therefore, the government should consider the following steps.

First, it should impose very strict rules and regulations concerning speculation generated by rumours. Those who buy shares, must retain it at least for six months before they can sell them, and if they do sell those shares before the due time, higher tax or levy would be imposed on them. This will gradually reduce the role of rumours in the stock exchange. Recently, it was revealed that a few people were caught for this act in the Union Paper Holding short-selling scandal. According to Islamic values a person is not allowed to sell something which he does not possess. It is indeed unlawful and unethical to do such a thing.

And second, to reduce the role of the stock exchange as the financial intermediary between the investors and the entrepreneurs. For an entrepreneur to mobilize funds, computer networking and information technology can bring the two parties together without any intermediary. The new formula will be partnership financing between the investors on the one hand, and the entrepreneurs on the other. The transaction costs will be removed and the profit and loss sharing will be introduced as an alternative. We cannot deny that partnership financing will bring stability not only to the financial sector but to the whole economy. This new formula of business enterprise known as partnership will forgo the role of the stock exchange as a financial intermediary, and can benefit not only the new parties but also the whole nation.[4]

Conclusion

Islam is not against speculation if it is made by genuine investors who have worked hard and analysed the macro- and micro-economic and financial fundamentals, and therefore have the right to speculate once the environment at the stock exchange is conducive to do so. On the contrary, what Islam is against is insider trading and the role of rumours, whose main interests are to manipulate the market and force their counterparts (the genuine investors) to sell off their shares at lower prices. Islam categorically condemns that, because such actions will undoubtedly bring harm to others and to the society as a whole.

Islam has clearly emphasized that for any financial transaction between two parties or more, a person should not do harm to others while others should not do harm to him. It is for the policymakers to examine the above proposal to promote the SMEs and make them competitive and efficient to achieve Vision 2020.

Notes

1 The views expressed in this paper are entirely mine and should not be taken to represent any official views or policies of any organization.

2 M.U. Chapra, *Islam and the Economic Challenge*, The Islamic Foundation and the International Institute of Islamic Thought, London, 1992, p.207.

3 Quran 2:205.

4 Saad Al-Harran, *Islamic Finance: Partnership Financing*, Pelanduk Publications, Petaling Jaya, 1992, p.377.

Chapter 12

The New Role of the Muslim Business University Students

SAAD AL-HARRAN

THE MALAYSIAN CORPORATE sector is booming because of various factors, especially sound economic and financial policies in the country and political stability. Although Malaysia has learnt some lessons from the Japanese experience in the development of small- and medium-sized industries (SMIs). It is argued that for the country to be fully industrialized, SMIs have to be well managed, efficient and competitive in the world market. It is not the abundance of money that makes SMIs successful and competitive in the world market, but rather the management of funds—and that is indeed a real challenge that faces the entrepreneurs in the new world economic order.

This chapter intends to analyse:

1. The historical background of the business and commercial scene in Malaysia;
2. The recent development of introducing entrepreneurship to the society to become part of the culture;
3. The characteristics of the typical Muslim business university student (MBUS);
4. The current problems facing the SMIs; and

5. The new role of the MBUS has been proposed to be considered by the policymakers and the corporate leaders.

Historical Background

Before Malaysia gained its independence in 1957, the Malays (or Bumiputeras, to be used interchangeably) were only involved in agriculture and rural farming and had little exposure to the new commercial activities in the towns and cities, whereas the Chinese had had tin mining experience as early as the sixteenth century, albeit on a small scale. With the discoveries of new tin mines the expansion of Chinese mining settlements was rapid. The Indians, on the other hand, were involved in the rubber estates. This phenomenon was reinforced by the British colonial policy to strengthen and maintain their power and influence in the Straits Settlements.

The above scenario has played (and will continue to do so for many years to come) a major role in shaping the role of entrepreneurship in Malaysia, that is, a large number of Malays are afraid to involve themselves in business, to avoid the risk of failure. Alternatively, they were trained to be government officers in the public sector. The Chinese were however trained to be in business to face the challenge of success or failure. Still, the government through the New Economic Policy (NEP) of 1971–1990 has played a major role in assisting small- and medium-sized Bumiputera companies to be successful. Yet the success rate is relatively low compared with the support that they have been receiving since the introduction of NEP.

Recent Development

The concept of entrepreneurship is indeed a new phenomenon in the Malaysian society. It was recently introduced by the government with the assistance of corporate leaders in the private sector as part of the privatization programme which the government has undertaken.

This entrepreneurship phenomenon is not only new to the culture of the society but also the terminology which came in with it, which is not well understood by many people. This kind of confusion of the concept of entrepreneurship and its terminology is not only in the context of the Malaysian experience but is also on the international level. This shows that although there is much interest on the subject much of the material is fragmented and highly controversial.[1]

This is why the government has paid special attention to developing the entrepreneurial culture in the whole society rather than parts of it. This shows that there is a gradual change in the Malaysian government policy towards SMIs, from one of neglect to one of promoting SMIs in recognition of its vital role in the overall economic development.[2] Therefore, the task that the government has initiated is not an easy one but the financial and technical support which it has extended to large number of SMIs has been encouraging their increase and growth. Today, many active Malaysian students becoming entrepreneurs (once they graduate from the university) instead of getting a job in the public sector. It is truly a positive development in the culture of the society.

Indeed, the government is determined to make the new phenomenon of entrepreneurship successful because the leadership has a long-term vision to achieve and that is to make Malaysia as a fully industrialized nation in the East in the year 2020. How far she has succeeded in her mission to change the culture of the society, the behaviour and the perception of the people. It is rather difficult to pass judgement (whether the phenomenon is successful or failure) in such a short period.

For any committed entrepreneur who has made up his mind. He has no other alternative but to commit himself to a long-term mission rather than any short-term gains. A commitment means to stay in the market and to be competitive rather than to be forced out of it due to various factors, mainly the quality of the product, price and service standards. To improve the quality of the production means that the entrepreneur has to work harder himself and with others. The others could be, the innovative and creative students who will advise (and be the future partners, once they graduate) the entrepreneurs. He has to trust them and learn from them the concepts of strategic management, marketing research and project financing to enable him to be competitive in the market. As for the students, they should gain precious experience from the entrepreneur and co-operate with him to make the enterprise successful.

Characteristics of the Muslim Business Student

The Muslim business university student is a mission-oriented person, inside and outside the university. His role and mission in the life is different from those of others due to his belief, commitment and responsibility towards the Creator, who made him a vicegerent on earth to serve Him (in this life) and mankind.

Allah says in the Quran: "He it is that has made you inheritors in the earth."[3]

Leadership

Various studies in Islamic management were conducted which support the argument that to be successful leaders certain characteristics need to be adopted. Among these are: intelligence, mission oriented, ambition, creativity and long-term goals.[4] To realize these objectives, the leader need to know the economic, social and political environment surrounding him to enable him to build a grass-root foundation. In Islam grass-root foundation is fundamental in building a solid society based on ethical and moral values. For Allah says in the Quran:

> Which then is best? He that layeth his foundation on piety to Allah and his good pleasure? Or he that layeth his foundation on an undermined sand-cliff ready to crumble to pieces? And it doth crumble to pieces with him, into the fire of hell. And Allah guideth not people that do wrong.[5]

The Prophet Mohammad (p.b.u.h.) was indeed a successful leader in terms of effective planning and organization of the Islamic state. His strong character, moral behaviour, humble attitude and love for others made him popular not only among the Muslims but also among the non-believers.

Allah says in the Quran: "Ye have indeed in the messenger of Allah an excellent exemplar for him who hopes in Allah and the final day, and who remembers Allah much."[6]

Trust (Amanah)

Our life is an *amanah* (trust). Allah has sent us (the human beings) as His vicegerents or trustees of Him on earth. We are responsible and accountable for whatever we do in this life. Therefore, integrity and trustworthiness in dealing with others, especially in financial transactions, is fundamental in Islam. The new role of the MBUS should enhance the concept of trust in dealing with others.

"We should not make harm to others while others should not make harm to ourselves."

Undoubtedly, the current corporate culture due to the deterioration in moral and ethical values need an urgent Islamic inputs. Trust in dealing with others has become a scarce resource in society. The students who are mission oriented in this life can play an important role in this direction.

Moral Values

Islam has stressed the importance of the moral and ethical values in the society without which no progress can be made. Indeed, moral and ethical values is to be considered the grass-roots for any society to prosper. It has clearly been stated in the Quran:

> Seest thou not how God set forth a parable? A goodly word like a goodly tree, whose root is firmly fixed, and its branches (reach) to the heavens. It brings forth its fruit at all times, by the leave of its lord. So God sets forth parables for men, in order that they may receive admonition.[7]

There is no doubt that we are living in a world of moral decay as long as such problems persist. There can be no prosperity and security in the society even when that nation has achieved higher level of economic development and rapid industrialization. The current financial crisis in Japan (and other parts of the world) has supported this argument. Many writers in the Western world have expressed their concerned about the moral decline in the American society. Every day the news is full of stories about business impropriety, employee theft and drug use, government scandals, teenage pregnancies and a host of other problems associated with the lack of morals and ethics.[8]

Sharing and Caring

In the world today, people —both the businesspeople and the consumers—are becoming more selfish, more individualistic, and are worshipping the wealth rather than Allah who has created it. We even neglect our parents, spouses and children in our pursuit for material gains. This kind of life has made us miserable with ourselves and towards other human beings. Therefore, there is no more care for others in the society. Even the relationship between the employer and the employee is not based on fairness and justice but on exploitation, unfair wages and salaries and hatred.

With this unhealthy financial world, we are of the opinion that the MBUS should play important roles in the corporate sector by introducing the Islamic concept of sharing and caring for others. They should be mission-oriented contributors rather than sleeping partners. Their mission should be active participation in the affairs of the society. Therefore, the MBUS should undertake an applied marketing research (under the supervision of their professor) to understand the consumers' needs and wants. Undoubtedly, an applied marketing research would help the entrepreneur learn from his previous mistakes. It will also assist him to make sound planning and monitoring of his line of production and give him feedback on any product that is not marketable: he has to know whether it is because of poor quality of production, uncompetitive pricing, poor management or something else. Indeed, it is only through sharing and caring that the two parties (the students and the entrepreneurs) will learn.

Current Problems of the SMIs

In the course of our discussion, we have to examine why SMIs in Malaysia has not been as successful as expected. There is no doubt that there are many problems confronting the Bumiputera entrepreneurs in business, of which the main ones are listed below.

Culture

The culture and the tradition of a society often directly influence an entrepreneur in his day-to-day work. The culture of avoiding business venture due to fear of failure need to be changed. It is indeed on the contrary with what Islam has advocated us to do: be in business rather than escaping from it. It is therefore important to introduce the concept of project financing to the culture of the Bumiputera society, and it is here the MBUS can play an important role.[9] By proper identification and selection of the projects (among other factors) successful will come if proper monitoring and following up are made by both the MBUS and the entrepreneurs.

Allah says in the Quran: "Never will Allah change the condition of a people until they change what is in themselves."[10] Islam encourages us to go into business and nine out ten of ones *rizak* (wealth) will come from business transactions. In many occasions Allah demanded that once prayer time is finished, man may disperse throughout the land to go about his business. And they who seek the bounty of Allah and remember Him frequently that shall prosper. Indeed, it is time to make changes in the Bumiputera culture and we are of the opinion that the MBUS can be agents of change in their society.

Lack of Ideas

The current Bumiputera entrepreneurs are lacking in creativity and innovative business ideas because of various factors, mainly the lack of proper education and exposure to other people. The lack of exposure in a manufacturing environment causes more damage than the lack of capital. One must know the industry well, the production techniques and the market before venturing into the manufacturing sector. Due to these factors, many Bumiputeras tend to follow others rather than to lead others. This kind of attitude have caused them to be left behind others in terms of improvement and development of projects.

Surplus Fund

There is no denial that SMIs were left behind previously when the government and financial institutions only extended credit to the large businesses due to their creditworthiness. But since the late 1980s, after the government introduced the privatization programme, the emphasis has changed. Nowadays, SMIs are receiving continual financial assistance from various government agencies. But the Bumiputera entrepreneurs still have a long way to go before they can manœuvre themselves into a position of greater competitiveness in the marketplace.[11]

As mentioned in earlier chapters, we are of the opinion that the problem facing SMIs in Malaysia is not one of the lack of fund but rather the surplus of fund. This scenario may vary from the rural to the urban areas. For the former it is indeed the lack of fund which has hampered many youths from starting their own business, but it is not the case for the latter. The real challenge is facing SMIs in the urban areas is not the mobilization of resource but the utilization of those same resources.

The New Role of MBUS

To enable us to bring changes due to the current problems facing the Bumiputera entrepreneurs, others (the policymakers and the corporate leaders) should realize that we are living in a world of rapid changes due to technological advancement and globalization. If SMIs (and Malaysia as a whole) want to survive in this competitive world then they should ask themselves questions such as those below:

a. How far have SMIs succeeded in penetrating the world market?
b. Have they really undertaken any marketing research to understand the real needs of their local consumers?[12]
c What kind of marketing strategies have they made so far if any?

d. Why have the local entrepreneurs failed to compete within each other in the country rather than outside world?

These challenging questions have indeed revealed some of the grass-root problems facing the SMIs today and in the future. We feel that serious efforts need to be made to change in our educational curriculum, in the business and the economic courses, to suit the corporate sector needs to realize the leadership's Vision 2020.

The students as main assets in the society who will make changes for development should be exposed to be part of the society rather than alien to it. Therefore, they should be exposed to real life experiences first by spending 24 months in the campus learning the theoretical foundations of some important subjects such as marketing, management, research methodology, business ethics, financial accounting, project financing, Islamic banking and corporate finance. Upon completing them successfully in the campus, the relevant professor (who will be assigned this responsibility) will identify and select some potential students based on various criteria. Some of these criteria should be based on the business ideas, innovation and creativity of the student (Figure 12.1).

The relevant professor should then have an open dialogue with selected entrepreneurs, especially those who want to improve their firms by being more competitive in the market. The open-minded entrepreneurs will accept the inputs of others, even if those "others" happen to be students who will be their future partners in the business once they have completed their studies in the university. An agreement should be reached between the relevant professor and the entrepreneurs for 12 months' practical training for the students, with their duties and rights clearly stated in an agreement which will be signed by their professor and the respective managing director of SMIs firms. Such an agreement or a memorandum of understanding (MOU) is indeed vital to protect the rights of the students now and in the future when they become partners in those firms later on. The MOU should clearly stipulate the following terms of references between the two parties (the students and the entrepreneurs of those SMI firms):

FIGURE 12.1
The New Curricula for Muslim Business University Students

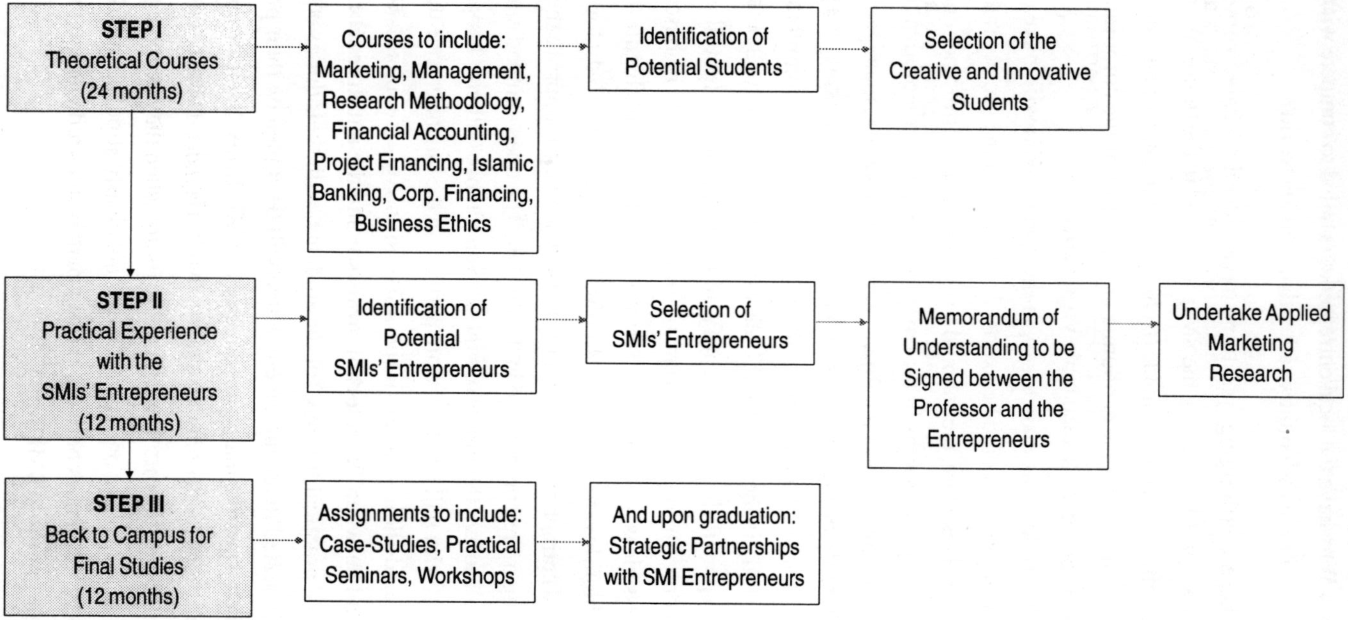

Sources: Prepared by Saad Al-Harran.

a. The students should spend 12 months in practical training with reputable SMI firms.
b. The students have to be closely monitored by the two parties (the respective new employers and their professors as well) about the conduct of their work during the practical training.
c. Confidential reports must be submitted every quarterly by the managing directors to the professor about the performance of the students.
d. The MOU should clearly state that if a student's performance during the 12 months is outstanding, he would be considered for partnership in that firm once he completes his studies successfully.

Undoubtedly once a student realizes that he may become a partner at the firm that he is currently helping out,[13] he will commit himself to the firm's success; while the firm will realize (later on) that their decision was the right one. The students are the new blood and should be considered assets in the organizational set-up now and in the future. They will make sure that they will give the right advise to their counterparts. The managing directors of SMI firms should take their new partners' advice seriously. The profit motivation will make them work hard.

Once the students have completed their practical training and gained real-life experiences. They would undoubtedly become a valuable assets not only to the SMI firms but also to academic institutions.

The MBUS should then return to their campus and complete their final or fourth year of studies, where they should to be given the opportunities and the responsibilities to make some presentations about their 12-month practical experiences. Their respective professors should give them the responsibility to conduct case-studies, practical workshops and seminars under his supervision. For students to be responsible is something new and awesome, they would need to be encouraged. It means that their respective professors would be moulding them indirectly into future corporate leaders that the Malaysian leadership is looking for, that is exemplified by the second companion of the Prophet Mohammad (p.b.u.h.), Umar bin Al-Khattab, who developed "Leader among the Leaders." This kind of practical inputs from the university business students is urgently needed. Their inputs after 12 months of practical training and experience will have important policy implications not only to the higher learning institutions but to the whole nation, whose leadership wants to make fully industrialized. The question should be asked as to how far is the current education system relevant to the corporate sector's needs and whether it is the right time to make some changes and modifications.

The culture of trust, faith and honesty in dealing with others are urgently needed in the contemporary corporate sector and we are of the opinion that the Muslim business university graduates can play (and will continue to do so) an important role in bringing changes to the corporate culture, which has suffered many setbacks because there has not been any moral and ethical values to control the human conduct, as evinced in the current financial scandals in Japanese corporations. It is an indication that we are living in the age of corporate crisis, corruption and financial scandals and moral decay not only of the corporate sector but of the whole society. Malaysian leaders have realized that we are living in the age of computers and information technology (which permit companies to access large amounts of diverse data, analyse, interpret and transmit around the world) and globalization (which means that the number of competitors with a worldwide reach is increasing, and markets that were traditionally considered impenetrable are slowly opening up to competition from other countries).

Conclusion and Recommendations

In view of the above scenario, there is an urgent need to formulate new education curricula for the business (and engineering) university students to cope with the rapid changes in the corporate world. We are living in the age of globalization and corporatization, and how far Malaysian entrepreneurs will succeed in penetrating the world market is indeed questionable.

This is why the Minister of International Trade indicated recently that the main problems facing the SMIs in Malaysia is the lack of research and development and productivity. We believe the Muslim business university students can play an important role in marketing research by changing the direction of the local entrepreneurs. We hope that the proposal put forward in this chapter should be the starting point for our policymakers and the corporate leaders in the Muslim world to examine critically.

Truly, we are living in the age of the corporate world, and business competition has become a weapon not only at the national level but also at the international level. Therefore, local entrepreneurs will have to face the reality of the new economic order by working harder with others based on trust, honesty, sharing and caring for the society and the strategic partnership alliance. The partnership should not only be at the national but also at the international level and this is where the marketing strategy comes in.

Notes

1 J. Cunningham and Joe Lischeron, "Defining Entrepreneurship," *Journal of Small Business Management*, 29 (1), January 1991, pp.45–46.

2 C.P. Lim, "Study and Evaluation of Existing Fiscal and Financial Policies and Support for Small and Medium Businesses in Malaysia," pp.57–58, in K. James and N. Akrasanee (eds.), *Small and Medium Business Improvement in the ASEAN Region Financial Factors*, Field Report Series No.16, ASEAN Economic Research Unit, Institute of Southeast Asian Studies, 1986.

3 Surat Fatir 39.

4 A. Abu San, "Administration in Islam," Modern Publisher, Dubi, UAE, 1986, pp.111–117.

5 Surat Al-Tauba 109.

6 Surat Al-Ahzab 21.

7 Surat Ibrahim 24–27.

8 M. Yousefi and K. McCormick, "An Assessment of Ethical Attitudes towards Wealth Accumulation," paper presented at the Third International Conference on Ethico-Economics, University of Cape Breton, Nova Scotia, October 8–9, 1993, pp.1–2.

9 S. Al-Harran, "Partnership Financing: Helping the Poor to Help Themselves," *The Bankers Journal*, Malaysia, October 1993.

10 Surat Al-Rad 10–11.

11 R. Ali, "Enter a New Breed of Bumi Traders," *New Straits Times*, Kuala Lumpur, November 27, 1993, p.12.

12 S. Al-Harran, "Islamic Consultancy House: Missions and Objectives," unpublished paper, Malaysia, December 1993.

13 S. Al-Harran, *Islamic Finance: Partnership Financing*, Pelanduk Publications, Petaling Jaya, 1993, pp.337.

The Contributors

Saad Al-Harran, the editor of this book, is an assistant professor of Islamic Banking and Finance at the Faculty of Economics and Management, International Islamic University, Malaysia. He is the author of *Islamic Finance: Partnership Financing* and the co-author of *Islamic Marketing Strategy: Eradicating Rural Poverty in Malaysia*. He obtained a Ph.D. in Economics at Durham University, England and was formerly the Operations Officer of the Islamic Development Bank in Jeddah, Saudi Arabia.

Rodney Wilson, Reader at the Department of Economics, Durham University in England, is a scholar of Islamic finance. He has published many books and articles, among which are *Banking and Finance in the Arab Middle East, Financial Development of the Arab Gulf: The Eastern Bank Experience, 1917–50, Islamic Banking in Jordan,* and *Gulf Trade and Finance*. Dr Wilson is also the editor of Islamic Financial Markets.

Radiah Abdul Kader obtained a Ph.D. in Economics at Durham University, England in 1993 and is currently a lecturer at the Analytical Division, Faculty of Economics and Administration, University of Malaya.

Wong Choo Sum is a graduate of the Business Department, Faculty of Economics and Management, International Islamic University, Malaysia.

Index